THIRTY STORIES

RICCARDO TONELLI

Thirty Stories

Pastoral Reflections for Educators

ST PAULS

Original title: *Trenta Storie da meditare e raccontare per un progetto di pastorale* © Editrice Elle Di Ci, Turin, 1998

Translated from Italian by Fr Stewart Foster

ST PAULS Publishing
187 Battersea Bridge Road, London SW11 3AS, UK

English Translation Copyright © ST PAULS 2001

ISBN 085439 606 3

Set by TuKan, Fareham, Hampshire, UK
Printed by Interprint Ltd, Marsa, Malta

ST PAULS is an activity of the priests and brothers
of the Society of St Paul who proclaim the Gospel
through the media of social communication

Contents

Introduction

For many years I have been interested in pastoral matters, and especially the pastoral care of young people. I have also written about pastoral 'projects', pointing out needs, models and actions in this field. I have always taken a serious approach, as is the way with those employed in this type of work. This time the method chosen to offer a contribution to such study and research may appear unusual and somewhat strange: it is by telling a series of stories.

To undertake a particular project, even in the pastoral sphere, is a task requiring hard work and professional competence. Those who have tried it know this only too well. Consequently, the way of reasoned argument seems to be the best approach. But isn't it perhaps time for a radical change of perspective?

I want to give an explanation as to the reason for my choice and to justify the logic behind it. Such clarification is owed to the reader, whom I ask to adopt a conscious and critical response. Moreover, it will serve to give a fresh presentation of the point of view underlying my entire project.

Telling stories...?

In a time of crisis with regard to secure points of reference, the decision to set about telling stories does not seek to be a submissive or defeatist contribution to the conflict of interpretations. When seen in the midst of life and its hopes, such a hypothesis can appear to be a dangerous and unjustified renunciation. On the contrary, I am convinced that the narrative approach can represent a valid way of defending what we seek to protect. I know that not everyone will agree with this. Without going too deeply into the merits of the question[1], I will now give some consideration to this topic.

Responsibility and imagination

The surest way to learn how to use a piece of computer software is to read carefully the user's manual, in order to understand the programmer's way of thinking. Indeed, where everything is precise and clearly defined, the only practical way forward is that which tells you what to do and what to avoid. In the jargon used, this way of doing things is called 'denotative'. The denoted statement is without a doubt the correct suggestion.

On the other hand, whoever in the name of freedom and responsibility offers to contribute their experience and expertise to a project which is beyond what we already have, must choose a way which can at the same time guarantee all necessary information, knowledge of its limitations and provisionality, and the concreteness of its own existence. In this case the 'denotative' model (that of the computer programmer) is not really very useful. It is neither justified nor practicable. Something different must be sought.

In recent years many people have rediscovered a way forward in 'narrative' models, which are capable of furnishing all the information necessary to arrive at a precise objective with regard to individual responsibility and creativity. This model of communication also disseminates information; but it benefits from a very different form of logic, viz. the 'evocative'.

The difference is by no means negligible. The following example can help to clarify things.

Someone looking for a book in a large library can work through the index catalogue or they can seek admission to the place where the books are kept. Working through the catalogue, they can find the location card of the book for which they are searching. This will give precise information on how to find the book. One does not yet have the book in one's hand, but one is in a position to arrive securely at that goal. In this case, the relationship between the catalogue and the book is very well-defined.

However, someone who goes to the place where the books are stored possesses a more general type of information, knowing the layout of the library and the system by which the books are classified, and perhaps also knowing on which shelf the desired book is located. Looking for it, one comes across other books, which are hastily consulted. One can reach the conclusion that there are more up to date works available, or on the contrary, one is convinced that the original choice was by far the best possible. In this case the information leads to the book without the precision of the index catalogue, but it permits a direct experience of other books: this is the 'evocative' method.

Under the denotative model the book is found by making the necessary references which track it down among the many hundreds of thousands of other titles kept in the library. The index catalogue is an indispensable medium. This requires clear, well-defined and precise information, consistent throughout the whole catalogue. The catalogue informs us about the book in the denotative way. Under the evocative model the information (suggesting the route to be taken to reach the shelf on which the book is housed, giving directions amidst the labyrinth of the library) helps to sustain one's personal freedom and responsibility. Without it, the book could not be found, but it does not act as a substitute for the reader. It serves to organise the reader's research, assuring a result, unleashing creativity, competence and imagination.

Metaphors aside, embarking upon a particular project is something very definite, committed to fostering life and sustaining hope. Certainly, whoever wishes to help plan well cannot substitute himself for the reader. However, some information is thrown into the field of research: it cannot be that an operation upon which so many expectations and resources are focused can be left to chance. The narrative model, which prefers to offer information in the evocative style, is a suitable instrument. This is why I have chosen to narrate particular stories to assist those who have to engage in pastoral projects.

A 'therapeutic' tale

These notes open with a second remark which I consider to be equally important in justifying the choice of narrative models.

The texts which speak about narration and its function of fostering life and hope often cite a tale which originates in Hasidic literature.

This is the particular tale: 'A rabbi, whose grandfather had been at the school of Baalshem, was asked to tell a story, one which must be told so as to be of help. This is what he said: My grandfather was paralysed. One day he was asked to tell one of his master's tales. And then he set about telling a story like the holy man Baalshem, who skipped and danced as he was praying. My grandfather jumped to his feet and began to tell his story. But he was so carried away by the story that he even had to do as his master did, singing and dancing as well. And so, after an hour, he was healed. This is the way to tell stories.[2]

The rabbi's tale bears a very strong therapeutic function. It restored the poor paralytic to the full use of his legs, to the point of being able to jump and dance. Is this an anomaly, or could it perhaps represent the normal function of every good story? It is certainly not easy to answer in the affirmative when one is faced with physical malady. Instead it could represent a fairly normal model, when the reasons for the disease are interior, linked to a disfunction nestling in the most intimate recesses of a person's life. In fact, the story assures an experience of great hospitality... and the perception of being welcomed unconditionally often results in interior change. Whoever takes up such a suggestion is easily tempted to impose himself upon his listener. This often leads to a crisis with regard to a long list of requirements to be respected or the burden of technical expressions. This no longer alarms us because we have learned to protect ourselves against these intrusions. We do not set too much store by these or treat them as one of many considerations, allowing them the right to speak only if they agree to propounding things which are unimportant. But even in this case the result is less than happy, because we remain prisoners of the very situations from which we must escape. Can we imagine a way of doing things which can hasten a real transformation and at the same time trying to secure a deep acceptance?

The story bids us to face the truth and its demands. It upholds, defends and promotes that truth, doing so with the strong sign of authoritativeness required of those who engage in this process. It is in fact a question of straining to go beyond what has already been acquired so as to add a personal touch to the world of the unpublished word. That word, which has its own requirements and demands, is not spoken except in a firm, sure and authoritative way, beginning from the claim that the things that are said are 'true'. Whoever seeks to tell stories hastens interior change, in the very same story testing the new situation towards which we are drawn.

True story-telling is in fact an advanced form of hospitality. Hospitality, promoted and tested in the style of communication used, 'interprets' the contents circulated, rendering them meaningful and true. This is not an attempt to hide the differences nor to trivialise the responsibilities involved. It produces new, positive situations, restoring the person to joyful knowledge of his or her own dignity.

Thirty stories

The second specification regarding 'stories' is this: their quality and, indirectly, the curious way of reaching the number 'thirty'.

Whoever examines the table of contents and starts to count the number of stories will find only twenty-seven. Yet the title of the book promises thirty. The numbers do not add up. For some readers, easily pleased, this does not present great problems. They know that 'thirty stories' could mean 'a certain number': more than ten and a little less than one hundred. But it is not like this. In the book 'thirty stories' means exactly thirty, not one more nor one less, but thirty according to a somewhat unorthodox calculation. The number is in fact reached by a special method of counting: $30 = 27 + 3$.

Twenty-seven stories are told. The three missing ones criss-cross the others like a kind of watermark. Told within the weft of these other stories, they are so important that they give meaning to the whole enterprise.

The choice of the 'narrative' model as a way of proceeding, and the telling of 'stories' (in other words, of parts of life), as the object of the narrative, not only serves to place life at the centre of the exchange of information, but involves it in an original way. Indeed, the narration interlaces three elements: the demands of life; the experiences of the narrator; the expectations, disappointments and hopes of the interlocutors. Each story, well told in the interests of life and hope, is always a type of synthesis of three different stories.

As I have mentioned, whoever seeks to help foster life and strengthen hope cannot remain silent about needs that go far beyond our subjective experience, even if all this rebounds upon whoever is speaking as something disquieting and provocative. The narrator does not therefore succeed by speaking as if he had not entered the fray and was by now beyond it. Life is an adventure of profound and continuous solidarity: only by welcoming this disquieting and yet reassuring involvement does he succeed in acquiring the authoritativeness needed to speak such demanding words.

Those who are involved in story-telling are not the passive recipients of what is offered, driven to communicate only from motives of convention or constraint. They are related to the development of the narrative, precisely because it is concerned with life and its demands. In every good story such things are spoken about in the first person, their hopes and plans, even when something is narrated concerning men and women submerged in the mists of time.

So much for the three missing stories: twenty-seven are told; three are woven into each of those narratives.

In this book the stories that form the hidden watermark are quite clear: the story of Jesus of Nazareth and the faith that he stimulated in his disciples; my own experience, hopes, disappointments, dreams and expectations, and those of the friends with whom I have for years shared my research into new behaviour and language so that the Gospel may still resound as good news for life and hope; the lived experience of very many people who, with a never-ending zest, take great pains in this fascinating adventure to serve the path of life in the name of Jesus, and that within the unique zeal of the ecclesial community.

The first story (that of Jesus and his disciples) is clearly present: it speaks of him continuously. In fact, the stories are almost all taken from the Gospel, at least indirectly. I could not have done otherwise, since we are seeking ways of continuing to realise Jesus' plans in our own times.

The second story (my own)... I must excuse what is perhaps too invasive a presence. But I could not have narrated the Gospel without relating a little of my own life.

I really do hope that the third story (that of the reader) is truly present... otherwise I would have been labouring in vain.

Which instrument?

The final specification concerns the significance of the instrument chosen. How can stories be used 'for' engaging in pastoral work?

Every reader is asked to respond. I too have my own response. Before presenting it, I feel the need to express my perplexity.

Often, when talking about pastoral matters and pastoral ministry among young people, I tell stories of the kind collected together in this book. I do so from the convictions already outlined. At various times friends have suggested that I might publish these stories. For a long time I resisted: I was convinced that the stories were made to be told out loud. Only in the telling of a story is it possible to restore to the event narrated the liveliness that comes from the participation of the story-teller and the attempt to involve also those to whom the story is offered. A written text perforce becomes a concentrated form of all these elements, once and for all. If the stories relate to the texts endowed with a special degree of authority (e.g. those referred to here) it really is fruitless to substitute them with something far more questionable and not even have the sense to add useless and irrelevant details. I gave in to the pressure after having established the favourable response to the publication of some of these stories in the journal *Note di pastorale giovanile*.

I have admitted this perplexity because it helps me to express the significance and limits of the instrument offered and, above all, to draw up some precise conditions that can make it work.

Stories for meditation

The stories told in this book are the fruit of prolonged meditation on the Scriptural texts cited, indirectly at least. I say this because it is the basis for the first indication about the meaning of the whole enterprise.

14

Whoever meditates on texts wherein one can recognise a normative activity for one's own existence is not restricted to trying to understand its meaning (important as that is), but goes much further. One's life is reviewed in the light of the documents meditated upon and one's experience is considered with those with whom one is in daily contact, in order the better to understand the text and one's own experience. Here too is proof of the value of stories constructed from the interaction between three different stories. Meditating upon the Gospel – the recollection of one engaged in the task of evangelisation – we move spontaneously towards pastoral action. Such reflection stimulates ideas for new pastoral initiatives.

I admit that in all this I have often been a little more reconciled to my own experience after having discovered the Gospel's unexpected capacity for hospitality and, at the same time, I have found myself deeply disturbed by the easy misunderstandings (personal and collective) with which now and again the demands of the Gospel are betrayed.

This is how the stories told in this book came about. With this intention they are offered to the reader. The invitation is to meditate on them, moving continually from the Gospel stories which inspire them to one's own personal story. I and the friends who appear throughout the stories wish only to suggest a need and to help to meet it.

Stories to tell

It is certainly true that personal meditation gives rise to the wish to tell others what one has experienced and discovered, thereby lengthening the chain of narrators. But it is also quite true that the stories cannot be told by reading them as if one was reading the texts like a letter. Real story-telling requires the restoration of the original narrative structure to the written text.

There are many ways of doing this.

If the tale is directed towards a reader, it can be meditated upon and rewritten as one likes, in order to gather together those details that seem more interesting and to add them to others so as to create a new kind of personal story. Each of these stories will then be able to be told to others, enriched by personal contributions.

When the tale is directed to a small group it can first be read, then meditated upon and re-presented through everyone's contribution. The stories told in this book must above all serve to facilitate the desire to continue story-telling 'to foster life'.

Many of us have learned to tell stories precisely by this sort of apprenticeship. The tales offered in this book can be analysed and dissected as one wishes, to meet the requirements of correct narration. Some suggestions emerge from the linguistic choices followed. A great many others spring from the abundance of stories[3].

From a 'responsorial' to a 'hermeneutical' usage

To explain the third condition I have used a cryptic title.

A 'responsorial' operation is carried out by one who responds to specific problems by making a choice from a ready-made repertoire. A 'hermeneutical' style is adopted by those who seek to represent whatever is offered, discerning between what is permanent (a type of 'hard kernel' which has unchanging requirements) and what is linked instead to particular cultural conditions. My own suggestion is based on this distinction.

Biblical texts (from the Gospels principally) are at the heart of the stories told in this book, being their normative point of reference. These texts have been selected. Why these and not others and why is there an emphasis on certain details and not others? The answer comes immediately from what I have outlined a little earlier: in the story narrated my own personal story and my theological and pastoral sensibilities are ever-present.

But there is more than that. The presence of the narrator does not only influence the choice of details. Many stories contain a series of extracts from the Gospels which do not correspond to the chronology of the biblical text. I have made a type of 'theological synopsis', gathering together events, precepts and details spread throughout the text according to a different spatio-temporal structure. This is also part of my story, the second of the three stories narrated within the one story.[4]

By what criteria have I made this two-fold selection? I must be quite clear, because I wish to recommend using the stories in a way that is in continuity with their origins.

The long involvement of friends engaged in day-to-day pastoral work has helped me to draw together problems and expectations, worries and hopes for the future. With these 'challenges' I have meditated on the foundational experience of every effort at evangelisation. I have tried to relate specific moments of this experience in order to show how it can be faced and resolved today as well. I have not made a 'responsorial' reading of the Gospel text, but a 'hermeneutical' one: I have thought about it and meditated upon it from the perspective of what appears particularly urgent.

How are the stories to be used with regard to pastoral work? The answer is obvious, following the previous statement: reconstructing the plot or weft with which they (the texts) have been written. In other words it is a question of reading between the lines of the stories, to grasp the problems and perspectives of today, meditating on the Gospel in the light of these challenges and seeking solutions that are in keeping with our own times in complete fidelity to the original event.

The narrative method is excellent for achieving all this in a wise and proper form. Story-telling stimulates, urges and challenges... in a good way: like two arms outstretched in a gesture of unconditional love and effecting a change of lifestyle even among those who had no intention to change.

I hope my own stories will have this result too. In fact I have told them only to restore the experience of God's welcoming embrace given by Jesus to all who approached him and, at the same time, giving rise to an unsettling wish for radical conversion to all the requirements of life and hope.

I know that this is no small claim. Let us try this together. I can also record some results in the direction hoped for.

Riccardo Tonelli

NOTES

1. I refer the interested reader to the following publications: R.Tonelli, A.L.Gallo, M.Pollo, *Narrare per aiutare a vivere. Narrazione e pastorale giovanile*, LDC, Leumann 1992 (includes a full bibliography); M.Pollo, R.Tonelli, 'E possibile educare narrando?' in *Note di pastorale giovanile* 31 (1997) 6 (contains a bibliography on the educative use of narrative).

2. M.Buber, Preface to *I racconti di Chassidim*, Garzanti, Nilan 1979, 3-4.

3. To assist such research, I give some recommendations for narrative syntax.

   With regard to the person of the narrator:

   • the narrator is a witness: he tells stories which have had a saving effect and which have been given to him, permitting a deep involvement in them;
   • the narrator is 'only a servant' of the story he tells: he tells it as it is in itself, even if it disturbs him, he tells it with a concern to put the story before himself;
   • the search for 'truth' always ensues, even if the narrator is preoccupied with an impassioned and significant truth, and thereby takes the liberty of transgressing a literal truth;
   • the telling of stories from the Gospels is the gift of the ecclesial community to those who search for life; the narrator lives out a true experience of the Church and joyfully accepts all its consequences (he does not have his own message to communicate, he looks for sharing and partnership, recognising the demands of a content which comes from beyond himself, he loves and welcomes the truth of the faith of the Church...)

Other recommendations give more explicit emphasis on some important details for making a real space in the personal story of those to whom the narrative is offered:

- the narration of a story imagines the language of the one to whom the story is directed, relating to the specific recipient and based on the rhythm of the narrative itself;
- the strength of the story is in its symbolic capacity. This is sought, carefully avoiding whatever diminishes the evocative force of the symbol (excessive realism, powerful channelling towards preconceived meanings, 'closed' and forced conclusions...);
- the narration of a story 'educates' those to whom it is told: it welcomes and inspires them, it challenges them and encourages them to move towards a sure process of maturity, it stimulates and fascinates while carefully avoiding any form of manipulation;
- story-telling seeks to restore each person to that interior solitude where the voice of the Holy Spirit speaks to them and where people make important decisions affecting their lives.

Good story-telling requires careful selection of what is narrated:

- narration is itself a message: the stories chosen are those which can most easily become a message and are told in a way which assists their interior application as a message;
- the message must spring 'naturally' from the story. It does not make complete sense to end the story with an explanation and interpretation, to draw a conclusion;
- the narration of a story is never reduced to a spectacle and above all it avoids whatever might be done simply for effect;
- narration seeks to evoke a response: for this reason space is left to the power of imagination, even if the very structure of the story constantly relates it to the event which we want to consider;
- it avoids everything that might result in distraction: excessive and useless repetitions, the uncontrolled welter of descriptive details which detract from the heart of the story...

4. This is not the appropriate context in which to defend the rights and wrongs of such an operation. It is simply my concern to make the consequences explicit. For a fuller treatment see: E.Schillebeeckx, *The Understanding of Faith*, London 1974.

1
Perspectives

First of all the perspective must be decided upon. This seems particularly strange when problems weigh down and there are so many things to do: the first really practical action does not consist in the task of achieving something quickly nor in the attempt to organise resources, but in settling upon the ideal horizon and direction. This is what the photographer does when wanting to capture a section of complex reality and enclose it in an image; it is what someone does when arranging a box of books on to two shelves as soon as they have been acquired. The same decision is offered to those who seek to engage in a pastoral work in a deeply pluralistic society.

To choose one's perspective means admitting to oneself and others where one stands amidst the many possible options, the dreams we have, who it is with whom we wish to work, towards which goal all our resources are directed.

In order to give some sort of answer to these questions I offer three stories:

Can we write new 'Letters to Philemon'?

Paul's Letter to Philemon suggests engaging the demands of faith in a courageous and innovative dialogue with contemporary culture.

Thank you, Nicodemus

Jesus demands a precondition (the 'new heart') for becoming people capable of recognising the meaning and the urgency of his mission ('life for all' in the name of the Father).

In the service of life

The service of life and the consolidation of hope are matters which truly affect everyone. They cannot be assured except by a deep and sincere partnership with all.

CAN WE WRITE NEW 'LETTERS TO PHILEMON'?

Philemon had a beautiful house, large and welcoming, a hoard of savings which allowed him to do as he wanted and, like all self-respecting property-holders, competent slaves who served and respected him.

Paul had converted him to Christianity on one of his journeys. With his conversion he had changed neither his house nor his customs. If he had kept his slaves and enjoyed his money, it was also because he had bought the former for a just price and the latter he had earned honestly. To the normal rhythm of his life he has added only a few more obligations... He has also become more honest in business matters, giving as much in alms as he can, loving those whom he meets and not treating his slaves too badly. His house was now that for all the Christians in the locality and for those passing through from other areas. Here they gathered to pray, to have a bite to eat and to celebrate festivals. As was usual at that time, the Eucharist also came to be celebrated in his house.

Meetings, feasts and Eucharistic celebrations were obligatory when Paul was travelling through those parts. Philemon looked upon him as a father, in the full sense of the word. This had nothing whatever to do with his parentage, but Paul had led him to discover the joy of the Risen One, he had opened his heart to life. He had truly given life to his spirit... and this was what counted the most. Philemon really did have the right to call Paul his father.

On that evening too, many people had gathered in Philemon's house to celebrate Paul's passage through the region.

They had eaten a large festive meal. Paul was at the

centre of the conversation. He was speaking about his experience of Jesus, of the great love that carried him through the world, with risks and dangers of every sort, to proclaim the Gospel to all. He could not remain silent about what was happening in recent times: Paul's enemies were increasing, he was feeling threatened. His former religious companions had not really forgiven him for changing his colours. Never mind... it was one thing to renounce the zeal of every good Pharisee... but to give himself to the enthusiastic preaching that the law no longer serves to give life and hope, because in Jesus alone can we be saved and set free... With these kind of ideas nothing would save him from meeting a bad end: it was only a question of time or opportunity.

On that evening too, as had happened on other occasions, before the final farewell, Paul consecrated the bread and wine and distributed it among those at table. In the bread shared the commemoration of the Crucified and Risen One became a saving event for everyone and brought with it new responsibilities. In this solemn and unique gesture, Christians know they are obeying Jesus' command, repeating the experience of Jesus at that famous meal, the last to be eaten with his disciples.

The story of Philemon is similar to that of so many other Christians: it reveals an important aspect of the life of the early ecclesial communities. That evening, however, something unexpected took place. It gave Paul the chance to write a letter of recommendation, and what is also important, gave us the desire to continue writing in such a way even today.

With a little imagination it is not difficult to envisage how something very upsetting took place that night.

Philemon had many slaves. None had contested his right to keep them: neither before nor after his conversion.

We know the name of one of them: Onesimus. He is the protagonist of the event which gave rise to Paul's letter to Philemon.

Paul was speaking. The guests were listening to him with great attention. He was speaking about wonderful things. Everyone was hanging upon his every word. But the slaves were thinking about their work. They were simply in a hurry to get to the end of the evening. They had to clear up, clean and tidy the house. Tomorrow morning it had to be clean and sparkling as always. By now the night was well upon them and the time for rest approaching.

But at a certain point Onesimus stopped what he was doing. 'What was Paul saying?' 'Come on, Onesimus, hurry up', said one of his unfortunate companions. 'Let me listen. Be patient... I don't want to miss what is being said.'

Paul was saying: 'Jesus, by his death and resurrection, has destroyed the wall that separated human beings one from another. Now there are no longer Greeks nor Jews, men nor women... there are no longer slaves nor free. We are all brothers and sisters in God's love.'

Paul's words rang louder and louder in Onesimus' heart. 'There are no longer slaves nor free... we are all brothers and sisters, all children of the same heavenly Father.'

But this cannot be. He is a slave. The memory of freedom was a long way off, linked to a lost world beyond the seas. He cannot remain in this situation. If God loves him, he has the right to be free.

By now the night is well advanced. Everyone is asleep. He got up from his bed and fled. He wanted to enjoy the freedom that God had given him.

He ran off with great speed, far from Philemon's house... But to where? A house of his own, fully free, that was beyond his reach. He did not know where to go.

He remembered Paul. He knew that he had remained in the city. He ran to find him and roused him from his bed. He introduced himself: 'I am Onesimus. I was a slave in Philemon's household. Your words led me to seek my liberty. Now I am here.'

He was waiting for anything. But Paul's words... he

rebuked him harshly: 'You cannot do this. Slaves must obey their masters. You must return to Philemon immediately. Straight away.'

'But you have said that there are no longer slaves nor free. We are all free. God has set us free. What now?'

Paul's reply made him very sad indeed. 'It's true… this is God's plan. Jesus has done it all. But now it is just germinating… like a tiny seed. Long winters must still pass before the seed flowers into a great tree. We must wait: be patient. Onesimus, you must go back.'

'I can't. Philemon will punish me. The law dictates the death of a runaway slave. I can't.'

Paul had no doubts. 'Philemon is a good Christian. Now… he wishes me well and owes me very many favours. Do not worry. I will write you a letter of recommendation. Go back to Philemon with my note and you will see that all will be for the best. But take this advice: obedience and respect for your master.'

Onesimus was persuaded to return. He had no other choice. His dream had been just like a flash of light. The night had returned, cold and dark.

Paul took a piece of paper and a pen and, in his own hand, wrote a few lines of recommendation. The document is recorded in the New Testament: the Letter to Philemon. He read it in an instant, all was fine, clear, full of love and encouragement.

'In Christ I have complete freedom to tell you what you must do. But I prefer to entreat you in love's name, I Paul, an old man, and now a prisoner for Christ Jesus: thus I implore you on behalf of my son Onesimus, whose father I have become in chains, who was once useless to you, but who is now useful to you and to me. I send him back to you with all my heart.

I would have been glad to have kept him with me, so that he might serve me on your behalf while I am imprisoned for the Gospel. But I did not want to do anything without your consent, in order that the good you do may not be by compulsion but of your own free will. Perhaps this is why he was separated from you for a while, but you have him back again forever; no longer as a slave, but much more than a slave, as a dear brother to me, but much more to you, both in the flesh and as a brother in the Lord.

So if you consider me your friend, welcome him as you would me. And if he has offended you in anything or is in your debt, charge it to my account. I, Paul, write in my own hand: I will repay it myself, to say nothing of you being indebted to me even for your own self. Yes, my brother, that I could have from you some favour in the Lord; give such comfort to my heart in Christ.'

The letter is touching. To people like us... it is surprising yet significant that Paul says nothing to Philemon about slavery. He does not urge him to grant liberty to Onesimus or his friends. He even refers to Onesimus as a thing to be coveted, as belonging to someone, to be given.

These cultural models frighten us. We have become too familiar with the Gospel to submit to such reasoning. But for Paul, as for the people of his day, things were straightforward. It was part of contemporary culture: that 'flesh' in which God was made visible to become our Lord and Saviour.

But this is such great news, as great as the abyss of love. Without questioning the perverse logic of slavery, Paul speaks about himself, Onesimus and Philemon with a tenderness which reveals God's love for us.

This is the beauty of Christian experience. The Incarnation is always redemptive. Assuming our lowly flesh, God passes from death to life.

For this reason God's love, planted at the very centre of our problems, exposes them and disperses all the contradictions. Christians began to understand such problems and contradictions and fought against slavery and other forms of cultural and social discrimination.

And what if we were to try to write such a letter to Philemon today... in an era when many of the cultural models in vogue fill us with fear so that we do not know where to turn?

THANK YOU, NICODEMUS

Nicodemus was an honest and cultured man. He had had enough of what was happening and anxiously awaited someone who could bring a little peace, tranquillity and trust. He had heard a lot of good things about Jesus. Who was to know whether he mightn't be the prophet so long awaited? To be honest, he was even a little hopeful: the words and actions of Jesus gave hope to the human heart.

But Nicodemus preferred to stick to what was safe. He was a man of experience and knew too much to allow himself to be taken in by something done for effect.

One day he plucked up courage and decided to meet the challenge. He went looking for Jesus. He found him and calmly took him aside. He put to him the questions which had been troubling him for some time: 'Master, you do marvellous things. The people follow you and they trust you. Tell me the truth: who are you? What are you looking for? What have you come to do?'

His questions were sincere. The words fell from his lips with a quiver, like those that come straight from the heart. 'No one can work marvels like you, unless they have been sent by God. Are you the prophet promised by God for the salvation of Israel? Is that it... or am I wrong?'

Jesus was soon aware of Nicodemus' sincerity. Nicodemus lacked just that final, decisive push before risking all. He was searching for it with all the trepidation and interior suffering that comes with every important choice in life.

If Jesus were to have given him a clear, affirmative answer, Nicodemus would have fired away.

Jesus wants to explore a little further. He had at last discovered someone with whom to speak about the mystery of his own existence. So he does not give a direct reply: that is too easy, even for someone like Nicodemus. Instead he draws him towards an even wider perspective.

He does not tell him who he is and still less what he has come to do. He says, quite bluntly, that for a greater understanding he needs 'to be born again'.

Poor Nicodemus was confused. 'To be born again... You must be joking, Jesus. I am old already... tell me how I can go back to my mother's womb.'

Realist as he was, Nicodemus was hoping for a change of direction. 'All right, Nicodemus, it's a turn of speech... Don't take me literally. Some banter at the beginning of the conversation helps to break the ice and for us to become friends... Now let's talk seriously: what do you want to know about me?' If Jesus were to have spoken like that, Nicodemus would have been ready to smile: 'Of course... you are a good fellow. Tell me now, who you really are?'

But Jesus does not withdraw what he said: he insists on going further. He renews the challenge to 'be born again'. But he explains that it is not a physical thing; it concerns the way one thinks. The mind and heart must change. Only someone who is prepared to change their way of thinking can understand God's plan, which Jesus seeks to reveal to Nicodemus. One cannot haggle over the conditions.

Jesus finds Nicodemus most agreeable. He knew what kind of man this good Israelite was, one who loved God, a faithful observer of the Law, able to run the risk for things that really matter.

He does not even seek to check whether he was ready for a change of mind and heart. That is certain. This was why Nicodemus had come. He had not met Jesus out of intellectual curiosity. He had not asked him crafty questions to put him to the test, as his colleagues had a habit of doing. Nicodemus seeks Jesus because he has some very important questions about life.

Jesus does not reply in the way usually reserved to those looking for popularity. In order to say who he is and why he has come, he reveals who God is and what his plan is for us.

The first reason is on common ground: that of the Law and the Prophets, in which Nicodemus is steeped.

Then all of a sudden, like a gust of wind that upsets everything we have carefully arranged on our work table, Jesus goes to the heart of the matter. 'Do you want to know who I am and what I have come to do? I will soon tell you. Have a new heart and you can understand.'

Here is Jesus' reply recorded in the Gospel of John: 'God loved the world so much that he gave his only Son so that whoever believes in him should not die but have eternal life. God has not sent his Son into the world to condemn the world, but that the world might be saved through him' (Jn 3:16-17).

He had reason to ask Nicodemus to change his way of looking at things. With the old heart, rooted in prejudice and full of fear, we cannot fully understand the message of Jesus.

The world that God loves is ourselves and all humanity. God loves our life and wants to restore it to the full (Jn 10:10). In order to do this he himself has come in search of human beings. He has become one of us, completely and utterly one with us. This is the great and unexpected 'Good News' which Jesus reveals to Nicodemus and, through him, to us.

Nicodemus, his friends and at least a few of us as well are used to separating good from evil and condemning the bad in order to make the good stand out all the more. We are sorry to find that the rain which falls from the skies and the sun which warms the earth do so with the same intensity upon both the good and bad. We would like a little more order and justice. Otherwise, in all this confusion which places everything on the same footing, it is not worth the effort to try to be good.

And then... there is no need to bring the excuse that it is not easy to distinguish the good from the evil. Nicodemus and the observant Jews had no doubt about this. They were the good ones... the admirable observant Jews. Everyone else was bad, without a shadow of a doubt. God knows how to sort out the good. Even with the language used for prayer and in the kind of money given as alms in the temple, God knows how to separate and make distinctions.

Jesus comes, steadily, to say the opposite. His words are hard. He upsets the peace.

God seeks life for all people. And for the bad as well? They are condemned, punished, excluded... others are restored to life.

God loves everyone and his love does not distinguish between the good and the bad. His love is not thus resigned. Things are not all right as they are. He knows that we are all filled with sin and death, even when we pretend not to notice. God's love is demanding and brings freedom. He loves everyone and restores all to life. Love is the condition for passing from death to life. Whoever returns to life can be loved unconditionally.

God does not turn a blind eye to sin, betrayal or evil. He loves the leper and restores him to unexpected health. He loves the poor prostitute and returns her to the dignity of a new life. He even loves Peter after his terrible denial and gives him back all the responsibility with which he had entrusted him before.

This is why God loves the good and the bad and seeks full and abundant life for all. Jesus has come to realise this seemingly hopeless task. Only one who has a new heart and a new mind can discover this, without being scandalised.

The story of Nicodemus really is one to put at the beginning of every investigation into the Christian life.

Thank you, Nicodemus.

IN THE SERVICE OF LIFE

This is the story of two disciples who, fortunately for us, have understood little about Jesus. From the very beginning they got everything wrong, and received a severe rebuke. Finally, however, they leave us with Jesus' teaching on the way in which we serve life in his name.

This is what took place... more or less.

Jesus had taught his disciples everything that lay in his heart. He had brought them into a lot of special situations. To them alone had he expounded some of his more demanding sayings. He had drawn them far away from the pressing crowds to give them time to think and to pray.

Now he left them to stand on their own feet a little.

He sends them on a journey, two by two. He gives them precise instructions: 'Look around you and do something. There is a great need for someone to stretch out a hand to the suffering, to restore some hope to those choked by the sorrow of desperation. Proclaim with courage that the kingdom of heaven is close at hand... Heal the sick and do good to all.'

Then, after a short pause, he continues: 'Have courage... go on your way. We will meet again here after a few days. We will share the experience of what we have seen. The adventures of one will be given to the other. My blessing goes with you.'

'What will you do in the meantime?', asks one of them. 'I will go off to pray', says Jesus. They go out towards the villages of the region.

They feel the responsibility of the solitude and the decision. The encouraging presence of the Master gives them strength.

The Gospel indirectly recounts the story of two of these disciples, because something special happened to them.

They came to the main square of a small village in the neighbourhood. They look around, with the curiosity that

Jesus had taught them. They soon notice a strange group of people. They go towards them, mixing with the crowd.

In the middle is a stranger; near him are two or three sick people on makeshift beds. The stranger is praying. Then he stretches out his hands. The sick jump to their feet, they are healed.

The people applaud. The relatives thank him warmly. Then, one after the other, they go off.

The disciples and the unknown healer are alone in the empty square.

With a knowingly look they then approach him. They greet him. They ask him point-blank: 'You heal people? In whose name do you do it? Have you heard talk of Jesus of Nazareth?' Faced with these questions, the stranger calmly replies: 'I heal the people... full stop. Jesus of Nazareth... I've never heard of him. Who is he? A competitor? I don't need any special recommendation. I lay my hands on people and they are healed. It seems that I am doing a favour to those who are suffering. And I am happy. Thank God for this gift... But why are you interested in all this?'

'This thing we have seen... here. You do not know us. We are disciples of this Jesus whom you say you do not know. He also heals. He has the right to do so. He has been sent by God for this.' They went on to insist: 'Look, you can choose. Either become a disciple of Jesus and continue to heal in his name; or stop healing people. It's prohibited... is that clear? Freelances are not welcome.'

The two disciples had been clear enough in what they had said. They went away satisfied, not worrying to find out whether the man had taken them seriously or instead continued on his way. They had done their duty. They had sorted things out and asked for change.

They were happy, and could report their success to Jesus. He would be happy with them. Poor Jesus, he really did deserve some consolation.

The episode finishes like this.

The disciples return. Before meeting Jesus they exchange

33

gossip with their colleagues. They found them discouraged and downhearted. They really didn't have much to report to Jesus.

Together they conclude: 'It is fortunate that you have something to say. Please... put in a good word for us.'

At last Jesus summons the disciples who had returned from their training exercise. Some banter is exchanged, a bit of a feast... and then Jesus asks, 'So, what happened?' The first replies are disappointing. 'Little or nothing.' Everything was routine.

'And you two... what have you to tell me?'

'Ah Jesus... we are happy. Something really amazing happened. We will tell you... you will see what consolation we at least will be to you.'

And they tell their story: 'We met a man who was healing the sick. He was very good... almost like you, when the crowd ask you for help. There were many people. There was no trouble we assure you.'

There is a short pause to catch their breath and to create a greater air of expectation.

'When everything was over we asked him if he knew you... if he had been your disciple... or at least if he was performing these good works in your name.' There is another pause. 'He said no, and in a tone which did not please us.'

'And you?' Jesus is in a hurry to get to the end, afraid that the jealous zeal of his disciples had ruined everything. 'What did you do?' 'Jesus, really, it is obvious. We ordered him to stop healing people. He could choose to come with us and become your disciple. He did not want to. Then we told him that was enough healing. We ourselves are doing it already.'

They were waiting to be congratulated and to receive applause.

Jesus is thinking quite the opposite. He reproaches them with an unexpected conclusion. 'You have understood nothing. Your way of thinking is terrible. People are not divided between those who know me and those who do not know me. This is what other rabbis do, but I am not like that.

I have everyone's life at heart. This is what I am all about: the love which fills my life and which should fill the lives of my disciples.

Finally... do we understand that whoever is for life is for me, even if he does not know me?'

The cause of life is so compelling that it seeks to be shared. Choices are made in life not on the basis of etiquette or formulae. The boundary lies between those who want life and those who take the side of death instead.

The disciples of the one who has made the service of life the 'pearl of great price', to gain which they are ready to lose all else, they are my companions.

2
Vocation

Every good plan begins and develops in an atmosphere of convergence of intentions and energy.

Its construction and realisation is always the result of collaboration. Together there is a growing awareness of serious and disturbing problems which have to be confronted, together we ask how we may become involved, and in real partnership the resources which allow change to take place are selected and organised.

In planning for pastoral work there is a much deeper reason for solidarity: we feel called by Jesus Christ, as 'his friends', to share his passion for life and hope for everyone, and to fulfil his cause with courage and competence.

Thus at the very heart of this willingness to work together there is an apostolic vocation.

The awareness and the quality of such collaboration is constantly judged, so that the knowledge of being 'but servants' of a higher plan is not reduced to work for its own sake, and so that they may attain the mystery of God and humanity.

To show that this is true, I suggest reading some stories which are at the very roots of the vocation of Jesus' first disciples.

The joy of following Jesus

Those to whom he entrusts the work of serving the kingdom of God, Jesus calls 'friends'. The readiness to work together in pastoral endeavours is the personal response to a demanding vocation.

Planning the way ahead

To engage in pastoral projects is a compelling task: it requires competence, courage and imagination. But this is not enough. To this Jesus adds the requirement of faith at least the size of a small mustard seed.

Faithful to the cause

Everyone usually starts off with admirable enthusiasm. Then the weight of time and problems slows things down and changes them. Mary's faithfulness is put before us... to discover a compelling need: the fulfilment of the plan comes before the claims of flesh and blood.

THE JOY OF FOLLOWING JESUS

Jesus was one of those rare people who when they have a plan in mind, think about it day and night and pursue it their last breath in order that it may be achieved.

His words leave us in no doubt.

Often those who listened to him heard him say things like this: 'I have come so that all may have life and have it to the full. 'Alas, there is still much to do to achieve that goal. Until then I cannot really rest.'

One day he drew a comparison which was far more valuable than any lengthy discourse: 'I am like that man who goes in search of pearls of great price. He runs here and there, not leaving it alone, because his passion is roused inside. If he gets to know that somewhere there is a very rare pearl, he hurries to get there first; he sells everything he owns to have the money available; then he happily buys the pearl he was seeking, paying no attention to the cost.'

The facts then took away any remaining doubts, just as the hot sun melts the last traces of snow. Every day was a constant race and the night was not long enough to finish the task. He and his friends were often forced to eat as they travelled along the road. He was continually approached by people who were suffering in body and spirit. He had a kind word for everyone. Many people returned home healed.

And then... the discourses that never finished, the heated arguments, the long hours spent in prayer.

Sometimes the disciples understood this passion and the reason for a life led with a burning zeal: the cause of life and hope for people in God's name. The Father had entrusted it to him; he had truly come for this purpose. Nothing or no one succeeded in stopping him.

There was so much to do. Yet his days were already numbered. He knew he was like a lamp whose flame was weakening because it had begun to run short of oil.

One morning the disciples get up early. They gather around him. He had spent the night in prayer. They were well aware of this because they had not seen him after the supper had finished. He calls for silence and their attention.

They are curious and impatient. They ask Peter and John, who usually knew about things a little in advance: 'What's happening?'. 'We don't know, we are going to see', the reply was immediate and sincere.

Jesus begins to speak. He gets to the heart of the matter straight away.

'The Father has entrusted me with an important and compelling task: he desires all humanity to have life and hope in his name.

We have done a lot together in these past few years. There is still much to do. We must go on. This is the point: you are my friends. I have chosen you personally, one by one, and I have shared with you everything in my heart. You really are my friends.

Well, are you ready to commit yourselves to my cause? You cannot waver nor seek to serve two masters. Faced with such a demanding task, you must choose: all or nothing. Choose.

I assure you: do not count the cost.

But let's be clear. I cannot promise you anything good. You will have trials. You will make a host of enemies. The work and the fatigue will deprive you of sleep and make you hungry. The cross will become your daily companion in life.

We have tried being together for the past few years. When one is involved in the lives of others in God's name, we are no longer master of anything: neither time, nor personal relationships, nor things. It is a fascinating life, full and abundant. Think of a mother who gives birth to a child. She suffers terribly, but she thinks of the life which she is bringing forth, and she is happy. The sight of life makes her forget everything. Even the memory of suffering is lost as soon as the new baby lets out its first cry.

You are my friends. I trust you so much that I entrust you with my deepest desire. There you have it. This is what I expect from my friends.'

They are dumbfounded. They were hoping for something better. They were ready to take risks on condition that there was something to gain and that they could begin to see something concrete take place.

The only tangible things Jesus promises make the flesh creep: sorrow, fatigue, persecutions. As for the rest, he asks for faithfulness: the joy that the new life will unleash when it comes.

Someone is tempted to compromise. He gambles on being subtle.

'Jesus, here I am, but first let me have a few days to think about it. You are asking me to do such a radical thing, give me time to check things out.'

'Jesus, I am coming. You have convinced me. But you know my father is ill. I am going to run home to see him. I am taking a few things and going back. Two or three days at the most, I assure you.'

'Jesus, you are right. What you are suggesting is good and attractive. I would be stupid to stand aloof. Tell me the truth: is everything in the future as bleak as you have made out? Just a small point... can we hope for the same today?'

Jesus' face looked sad: 'Possible? You have been with me for many months indeed... and you are still not free of the old ways. This is not where we really are. With this way of thinking we cannot serve life: absolutely not.'

He replies to the questions straight away. 'Do you know what awaits you? The foxes have their holes and the birds of the air their nest. I have nowhere to lay my head. The whole world is mine... because everyone has a great hunger for life and hope and God loves everyone and gives to all, both sun and rain. But I possess nothing. When you go out, take no supplies with you. Whoever serves life, lives with the risk of that service.'

Then, in the same manner, he engaged those who wanted to postpone their decision: 'We cannot wait. We cannot ask those who struggle under the shadow of death to be patient for a few more days, while we go to greet our friends or bury our dead. The cause comes first, even before flesh and blood.' He speaks with force. Someone thinks of Mary, his mother, mingling with the crowd waiting for Jesus, ready to wait for her turn, she who had a heart brimming with the desire to throw her arms round him after those long months of silence.

'Lord, you have convinced me. I am coming. I do not know you. But one who speaks as you do, I will follow him everywhere. I have finally found that bit of my life for which I have been searching and was not able to name.' Everyone turns towards the stranger who had joined the group without being invited. 'Who are you?' He replies, without a trace of shame: 'My name is Levi and my job is not a very nice one. I am a tax collector. I heard you speaking while I was going about my business. I listened to you and my curiosity soon turned to admiration. I'll come straight away.' He stopped for a second. Then he continued: 'Immediately, no. What you are asking me is terrible: to abandon everything – money, friends, job, to come with you to serve the cause of life. You do not promise me anything good. And yet I am coming. If you trust me and have the courage to call me your friend, then here I am.

Today the greatest adventure of my life has happened. I

am happy, like a boy when he falls in love for the first time. I want to shout to all my friends. Look, this is what I am doing: a big celebratory meal. I invite all my fellow adventurers, to tell everyone about the joy of giving up my wealth to remain with you. Can I?'

The disciples look towards Jesus. They expected him to say no. He had forbidden visits to relatives and returning home for a funeral. Shall we see how he gets out of this one?

They do not have to wait for Jesus' reply: 'Of course. Come with me... after the farewell meal. I do not want people following me with long faces. I want happy people. To break for a festive meal is fine. After that we will leave together.'

'Thank you, Jesus. That's settled, you are all invited to the farewell lunch. My friends must find out who this Jesus is, to whom I am giving my whole life.

The disciples are taken aback. What if Jesus were a little odd. They had already experienced this at other times. He got a frantic delight from turning their way of thinking upside down, such good and devout people who scrupulously observe the law. This time, however, he has gone too far: first he says no to someone who was seeking a short postponement in order to greet his relatives and mourn his dead father, and then he allows everything to one who suggests having a farewell meal.

Jesus reads their thoughts and continues his words: 'I understand, what has happened doesn't seem logical. And you are not completely wrong. But there is one thing in my heart and which I want to say, loud and clear, because it represents the way in which I invite you to serve the cause of life with me.' The silence returns.

'Try to think what the servants are called to do in their master's house. At the end of a day's work the master sits at the head of the table, but the servants are busy with a thousand tasks. They prepare the table, cook the supper, offer water for the ablutions... and then they bring the food to the table... they clean and tidy up the house. Finally, at the end of these tasks, they too can have a bite to eat, perhaps somewhat hurriedly because night is drawing on and the dawn will soon be up for them at least.'

The parable was clear, but what did it have to do with them?

Jesus continues, 'Who is more important: the master or the servant?' There is no question: 'The master, he has the right to behave in this way.'

Jesus looks at them. After a short silence he replies decisively: 'You call me master and Lord and you do well, because I am indeed. What am I doing with you? I do as the servants do in their master's house. I am among you as one who serves.

Do you know why? I do not want to preach to you... I simply ask you to pay heed to the important points.

The cause of life finds first place in God's heart: it is his desire and his pledge. He fulfils it; but he has entrusted it to me; I have entrusted it to you, because you are my friends.

When we have done all that we have to do, we must have the courage to recognise that we are only servants... without great pretensions. Now is it clear what the parable of the master and the servant means?

For life and hope... God alone is the master. We are only servants... very precious because the cause of life is entrusted to us, but only as servants, because God is in charge of things.'

They understood the parable and its conclusion. But there were still some doubts... about Levi's meal.

Jesus does not want to leave such an important argument hanging in the air: 'Do you want to know why I allowed Levi to delay his departure to arrange a festive meal?'

Two reasons led me to this choice. I will tell you: there cannot be secrets among friends.

The first is more obvious. By arranging the feast, Levi wants to express his joy at giving up everything to follow me. He is very good... he has understood fully the story of the pearl of great price. The second reason is also important. Try to think about it.

The cause of life is rooted in the mystery of God. We are sure of the result... only by faith. The meal is the most beautiful expression of our trust in him... Whoever takes part in the feast recognises that he or she is only a servant... at any rate that is true for those who entrust the result of their efforts to the mystery of God.'

I would have gone for the first reason... but the second is too cryptic for the way of thinking of those who are used to assessing everything by verifiable data. The disciples will discover this only when they begin to consider even the death of Jesus (and their own violent death) as a great feast of life and hope.

PLANNING THE WAY AHEAD

Jesus had explained to his disciples all that was necessary to go out into the world, with zeal and competence, to preach the Gospel.

He had told them that they must proclaim the Good News and he gave them the perspective to do it. 'I entrust you with glad tidings. Tell it to everyone. The people need it and anxiously await it. By now they are tired of listening to long sermons full of rules and prohibitions. Say this: the Kingdom of God is close at hand, indeed, it is already among you. It is a question of discovering it, of learning to look around you. The words that you speak must lead people to experience that God is a loving Father who wants life for all.'

Someone asked him, 'Who should we begin with?' And Jesus replied: 'The poor are the ones who have the right to receive this Good News first. They are usually last. They only receive good news from others, if someone takes pity on them and tells them what others, those who matter, already know by heart. Please, don't you do the same. Begin with the last. This way of doing things began the day I was born. I hope you have heard that said. The angels went first to the shepherds. This time, other people had to be told by them.'

Jesus, in the crash-course of training given to his disciples, had also taught some technical things. He wanted to defend the conviction that good will alone was insufficient. He had given this recommendation: 'Be careful not to be too wordy. The plain facts are the most convincing words, so begin with the facts: the lame were made to walk, sight restored to the blind, and the deaf can hear.' Then straight away he added these words: 'Be faithful to the one who has sent you. Do not take too many provisions. When you enter a house salute those who live there and invite you to eat: it is a form of payment for the service you give. In fact, you too are workers that have the right to a just wage; labourers of the Kingdom, but always labourers, who eat what they have earned, with the sweat of their brow. If someone drives you away, forgive him. You must change your lodgings without making a fuss.'

Jesus had explained everything to his disciples, just like a good master, happy to share his own wisdom with his friends in order to involve them completely in his mission.

They are now ready to leave, going into the world to preach the Good News. Jesus makes a final gesture of affection towards them. 'I will go with you for some of the way, would you like that?'

They were happy. To be with Jesus gave them security, even if they thought they knew everything, the unexpected might always happen.

They are in the main square of the first small town on their route. They soon notice a group of people in the centre of the square.

Jesus is not concerned and tries to go on along the road, as if those people should not worry him very much. With the piercing look that comes from a love and zeal for life, he had already noticed everything. He showed indifference in order to put his disciples' training to the test.

They had learned Jesus' lesson very well. 'Jesus, stop. We must go and see. You have taught us to be curious about life and hope for the people. We cannot go on without first checking whether any among the crowd needs us.'

'Well done!' says Jesus. 'Of course my disciples do not walk with their eyes fixed to the ground, as if nothing should interest them on account of having so many other things on their mind.'

Two go off purposefully. They go to see the people. They return a few seconds later, out of breath. 'We must stop and intervene immediately. There is a small boy among those people who is killing himself with his bare hands. He is frothing at the mouth and hitting his head against the pavement in the square, shouting like one possessed. His father is powerless. The others are frightened and do not know what to do. Let's go! Do you agree, Jesus? You have taught us that the good shepherd leaves the good sheep in the sheepfold and runs after those who have gone astray.'

This is a another great consolation to Jesus. He thinks to himself: 'my disciples really are good men. I can trust them. With people like this we can change the face of the earth. They have understood that one cannot be a disciple of Jesus and proclaim the Kingdom if one is without zeal, strength and single-mindedness for the cause of life and all its manifestations.'

The disciples of Jesus arrive. The crowd makes room for them. They take the dying boy by the hand, they call him by name, they do what they had often seen Jesus do. Nothing happens. In fact, it is worse than before. The people look at them menacingly. Then someone raises his voice: 'Go away, there is already enough confusion. Walk away and go back to where you came from.'

They return to Jesus. They are devastated. It had all seemed so easy. They were expecting the crowd to applaud them and the father to embrace them. Instead they have been insulted.

'Jesus, what shall we do? Please, you go. I have failed this poor lad. It's all yours.'

Jesus intervenes. He calls the boy by his name and raises him up with his hand. The boy no longer has convulsions. He is peaceful. He smiles. He is healed. He settles into his father's arms. Death has been defeated. Once again life has triumphed, thanks to Jesus.

The people applaud. The father thanks Jesus. He asks him how he might find him again, a little later, where in somewhat calmer circumstances he can express the gratitude of the whole of the boy's family.

Jesus speaks about the nearness of the Kingdom of Heaven, present among them. He points to the Father who is in heaven. Then he greets them and returns to his disciples. He is happy. Today as well he has proclaimed the Kingdom of God with forceful words.

Once more Jesus and his disciples took to the road together. But they could not leave things like that. They return to their intense course of training to become good evangelizers. Had they not asked for it themselves, Jesus would have surely intervened directly. What was missing was too important to leave things hanging in the air.

Someone plucks up the courage and asks the key question: 'Listen, Jesus, you have taught us so many things, but you have kept back some secrets. We are sorry, but this is not very thoughtful. If you want us to be your disciples forever and we are not to cut such a poor figure as we have done today, you must reveal this secret. How is it that you were successful and we were not? We did everything to heal that poor boy, but we did not succeed. You arrived, and all at once you gave him back alive to his father. Why? Where did we go wrong? What skill are we still lacking?

All of them say: 'Go on, Jesus, please teach us the final trick as well.'

Jesus replies without any half-measures: 'I have taught

you everything, I am not keeping any secrets from you, believe me. Yet why are the results so different? You have good reason to complain. You are lacking something and it is the most important thing. The skills that you have already acquired do not increase not because there isn't some additional technique available only to the initiated. Do you know what you are lacking?'

They all remain with mouths wide open in anticipation. Jesus stops for a moment, to force them to think and to pay attention to things beyond the concern for efficiency. Then he continues, using this little bit of imagination to say what was most important: 'You see that mountain over there?' Everyone turns round, with a question mark written all over their faces. 'Good, if you had faith the size of a grain of wheat – and you know that it is the smallest of seeds you would say to that mountain: 'move from here to there', and the mountain would obey and move straight away.

You were lacking in faith, the only thing which, in the end, really moves mountains.'

It does not take so much, Jesus does not suggest a mountain of faith to move a grain of wheat. It takes faith but even a little works great things: to pass from death to life.

Jesus' training sessions have finished. He has taught the contents, the perspective and the techniques: everything that is important, is sufficient to pass from death to life. They are not useless: on the contrary, you cannot really do without them. But they are not enough to solve problems. It takes faith, the decision to immerse oneself in the mystery of God, because only God truly passes from death to life and we, with all our sophistication, are only servants.

Now the disciples are ready to leave, with the diploma in evangelization in their pockets.

FAITHFUL TO THE CAUSE

Thirty years went by with Jesus sharing the same rhythm of life day after day. Mary was used to it. And she was happy.

There was the distant memory of what had taken place at Jerusalem, on the journey arranged for the celebration of Jesus' twelfth birthday. Every now and then Mary used to return to it in her prayers; she saw it as an omen of something that was to happen. But as time passed she became less worried. Jesus was happy and well, living at home with his mother. Nothing seemed to disturb the joy of their life together.

At first it was she who used to teach him the mysteries of religious experience. She used to tell him the wonderful stories about their people. She used the less happy chapters in that story to give him the advice which all mothers give their children.

It wasn't long, however, before their roles were reversed. Jesus had too many important things to say. He seemed to know, as if from direct experience, some secrets about the mystery of God. Every so often he even used to let slip calling him 'Father' in such an original style that was quite amazing.

At a certain point something changes. At first with some remarks and then with an even more definite tone, Jesus begins to speak of a great and demanding plan. He said: 'Mother, do you know what someone who seeks pearls of great price does? He looks anxiously everywhere; he searches for information; he thinks about it day and night. Then, when he gets to know of the whereabouts of a pearl of great value, he sells everything in order to buy it. This pearl is the dream of his life. Everything else counts for less: it is beautiful, interesting, pleasant, but the pearl, he loses sleep over it and it quenches every other desire.' He quickly added, looking somewhat dreamy: 'I have found the pearl of great price. I must go. I will soon give up everything. The Father has given me a task which is like the precious pearl.' Mary listened and pondered. She was hoping that that day would never come. She was wishing it was a long way off.

One day, all at once, Jesus embraces his mother, greets his friends, organises his few possessions, and leaves, with the enthusiasm of one who had finally found the precious pearl around which his whole life revolves.

The first few days had been hard for Mary. Without Jesus around everything seemed sad. The house was empty. A thousand things reminded her of her far-off son, lost in a peculiar and rather dangerous passion.

Mary knew how to pray. She had taught Jesus. So even now she reflected, meditated and prayed. In her prayer she discovered that Jesus' great enterprise did not involve her son alone. It was hers as well: a decisive part of her life. Jesus had bestowed upon her his passion for the pearl of great price.

The passing months seemed long.

Now and again, in successive waves, sayings and memories came back to her, filling her heart with joy. Jesus speaks words of peace and hope. He commits himself to the life of everyone. He even knows how to resist the pharisees and chief priests who acted like masters in the name of God. Those who had passed through Nazareth and had met Jesus in places trusted him. Now and again someone even brought her greetings from her son.

Sometimes a shadow passed through his mother's heart: 'let's hope for the best – striking at the powerful is always dangerous.'

One day she met a woman along the road. The woman was looking for her. 'Are you Mary? Are you the mother of Jesus?' She did not have time to say yes. The woman threw her arms around Mary's neck and kissed her on the cheek. 'Mary, thank you for having given us Jesus. My son had died from a mysterious and incurable illness. Think about it: ten years old, violently snatched away by death; and I am a widow. I was desperate. He had already been laid in the tomb. Jesus came like a ray of sunshine in the night. He stopped the funeral and called my son by name. Now he is alive. He is well. Mary, thank you.' She gives her another kiss, more solemn than the first.

Mary feels very moved. She shares her son's cause with the same burning passion. She felt him to be near, in the signs of life that his presence sowed all around.

But such nostalgia for Jesus. Is it possible that he might never pass this way again?

Then something good happened. One day a friend arrived at Mary's house like a bolt out of the blue. 'Mary, do you know that Jesus is in the area. He is preaching in a village nearby. Let's go to greet him. Are you coming?

Some hasty preparations, a few words to the neighbours, and they set off towards the place where Jesus was.

In the main square a large crowd had gathered. Jesus is in the middle of it. He is speaking. Mary stops at the edge of the crowd. She sees Jesus in the distance. She scrutinises him with a mother's look. He is a little dishevelled. But his eyes and voice: it is him alright. So many people are listening to him with joy and interest. It is beautiful the absence has been well repaid by the good that he is doing.

Mary waits. Perhaps Jesus has not noticed her. Wait. As soon as he stops speaking and has a bit of peace, the embrace will make up for all the waiting.

In the crowd there is also the woman whom Mary had met a few days before. Her son is with her: a fine looking boy, bursting with health.

The woman spots her. She comes forward. 'Mary, Jesus has not seen you. Call him. Go to the front. If he does not see you, he will continue speaking. You know I have been told, how sometimes he goes on until it is dark. He speaks so well. Everyone wants to listen to him. But time is getting on. Go forward.'

'It's all right. I'll wait. Do not worry. It's enough to see him from a distance. Jesus has got his duties. I cannot interrupt him.'

In her heart she was pondering the pearl of great price which Jesus had spoken about so much in recent times. She thinks about it, with joy and trepidation, while Jesus' voice sounds from afar.

The first woman comes up to her again: 'Mary, call him. Do not be afraid. He is your son. There are so many mothers here. They will understand.' 'No. Wait. Let him finish', Mary insists. The woman has had enough. Now she decides to act as a mother. 'Jesus', she shouts, plucking up her courage, 'here is your mother, a woman so fortunate to have a son like you. It's your mother, Jesus.'

Jesus stops for a moment. Everyone turns towards Mary. Someone urged them to applaud. Mary truly deserved it, with a son like this.

They did not have to wait long for Jesus' reply: 'Mary, my mother, has understood the story of the pearl of great price very well indeed. The cause of life for all takes priority over one's own flesh and blood. Mary knows this and has chosen it. Let us continue.'

Jesus' words seem hard and unbending. Mary understands them very well. She has perceived them for such a long time. Now she must choose. She reaffirms her choice to be faithful. And she waits, calmly.

The story of Mary's faithfulness to Jesus and his cause has a sad and violent ending: the cross. At the foot of the cross Mary, through her tears, once again reaffirms her fidelity. She does so on our behalf as well, to make known that it is necessary and to assure us of the outcome.

This is the faithfulness that serving the Gospel requires of those whom Jesus calls to share in his work: life and hope for all take priority, even before the ties of flesh and blood.

3
The Task

In every good enterprise there are two elements which are in continuous relationship: the objective which it is intended be achieved and the resources necessary to create the conditions which favour its achievement.

The word 'resource' refers to everything which can put at the disposal of one who undertakes a particular project. Some resources exist already; others can be easily assembled, unleashing imagination and zeal. Those resources which exist are evaluated in terms of being consistent with the objective. The invention of new ones is achieved by the same very attentive consideration of the objective.

All this applies to every serious project. It is remembered by those charged with putting it into effect.

In the pastoral sphere this operation is achieved by paying careful attention to a series of requirements that stem from the way in which Jesus and his disciples promoted the cause of life and hope. We certainly cannot re-create the exact conditions of the Gospel texts in the way we do things in the church today. But we must have the courage to examine our pastoral practice in the light of the challenge of the Gospel, to write a modern handbook for pastoral work, faithful to the present which has its roots in the past.

It is not an easy task. Difficulties come from two opposing perspectives: either we are embedded in what makes us feel secure so as to preserve the past in easy available terms, or we fail to have enough respect for human wisdom to make it the living flesh in which to allow the Gospel to speak afresh.

The following stories are an attempt to propose some of these 'links' between faith and culture, and suited to pastoral projects. They serve as examples of a task that must continue.

Peter, the man who was lame, and Jesus

Schooled by Jesus, Peter has discovered what is at the heart of serving the Gospel: to make the lame walk, telling them the story of Jesus of Nazareth.

Education in the law

To be challenged by the law is a fixed requirement of any pastoral project: it is important to be educated in the law, for the law is for life. The service of life is the basic criterion of the freedom brought by the Gospel.

Looking to the future

The disciples of Jesus are people who know how to keep watch, to make provision, and to organise themselves, not to remain outside the feast as happened to the five foolish bridesmaids. But to make provision for the future means it is necessary to anticipate in the present that solidarity for which we long, quite the opposite of what the five foolish bridesmaids did.

Ways of seeing things

Every good teacher knows how necessary it is to speak forcefully about the demands of life: it certainly can't be passed over in silence. There is another question: how are we to 'see things'? Nathan, who reproached David for his sin, still has something to teach us today.

Enough of materialism

Even in pastoral matters a materialistic way of thinking creeps in: if you do this you will gain a reward, something today and much tomorrow. This is why someone asks 'what's in it for me?' when faced with any proposed task. Instead how seriously do we take the model of the seed which must die in order to become a grain of wheat?

Who is the human person?

Every pastoral initiative begins from staking a bet on humanity. Who is the human person? A visiting card is not sufficient for identification. Jesus, urged on by his disciples, makes a very firm stand: between the type of person found in the Pharisee and that of the tax collector, he chooses the latter, without any hesitation. What about us?

Whose side are you on, God?

Those who engage in pastoral work turn to God and he gives them words to speak. God, who are you for me? Whose side are you on? What is your will? Jesus runs up against the doctors of the law and the sages of the temple because the image of God that was reflected by their behaviour was very different from the real one, which, one Sabbath, had allowed the sick woman to walk upright.

Self-giving love

The doctors of the law were expecting a list of people whom they should love and in due course a second list of those with whom they were not to concern themselves. Jesus turns things upside down: to love one's neighbour means 'to make oneself the neighbour', and so, in doing that, we turn towards God.

A significant experience

Jesus does not confront problems by 'discussing them' with his disciples. He chooses another route: he gives them the experience and then helps them to work them out. The Transfiguration is a momentous experience which becomes a means of telling who Jesus is and what he offers to all.

Wishing to see Jesus

The story of Zacchaeus is of great interest when conceiving

*the basic structures of a pastoral project: Jesus responds
to Zacchaeus' curiosity by asking him to be invited to his
house. Jesus' welcoming embrace leads to Zacchaeus
making a radical change to his lifestyle. Conversion is
born of acceptance.*

In favour of life... but how?

*We all have a great will to live. Jesus agrees: he has come
that all may live life to the full. But he says clearly that only
by running the risk of losing all, sharing everything with an
unlimited solidarity, can we all have life.*

PETER, THE MAN WHO WAS LAME, AND JESUS

After the Resurrection of Jesus, Peter had resumed the
custom of going up to the temple to pray, in blessed peace.
He needed to. The responsibility of the Church, which
Jesus had entrusted to him before he died, gave him much
to worry about. First, when the Master was still with them,
it was easy to understand him. He could even make mistakes,
and Jesus did not send word to him. Thus, between good
counsel and the proverbial blunders, he learned to be an
evangeliser at his own expense. Everything was more
complicated now. He felt alone, even if he was not without
the comfort of the other disciples, who were his friends.
Every now and then he even had to solve others' problems.
They came to him in no uncertain terms. 'You are the head.
Jesus has given you authority and responsibility. What
shall we do?'

That day had begun like so many others. Then, all of a
sudden, an unexpected happening had made it a special

day. The book of 'Acts' even records the exact location: at the Beautiful Gate of the Temple.

Peter was entering, preoccupied with his own worries. He was hoping for an hour's peace, in prayer and reflection.

On the threshold of the temple he finds the way barred by an outstretched hand. He stops immediately. It did not even cross his mind to speak to the poor man who was holding out his hand to him: 'Listen, I don't have time now. We will speak about it later. Let me pray in peace and then I will see if we can find a solution.' He still had not remembered everything that Jesus had taught him, but he had learned all about dealing with suffering. When someone is suffering and calls for help, this is the most important thing. Everything else takes second place. There is not time to discuss theories and seek clarification. One must intervene, well and good.

Peter stops. With a quick glance he takes stock of the situation. He does not want to leave on the wrong footing. He is afraid that the earnest zeal which Jesus had passed on to him could be playing cruel tricks.

At once he realises it: the outstretched hand is that of a poor man who was lame; he is asking for some money to get him through the day.

His reply is quite direct. He looks for some coins, but in vain. He is sad: 'I have nothing on me. I cannot help you.'

Something wonderful follows. He was wanting to say: 'Be patient, there will be another time.' But the story of the Good Samaritan struck a chord within him. He did not say to him: 'I will pray for you.' Jesus had never done so with those who were suffering and who asked him for help. He came up with a spectacular reply.

'Listen, I do not have any money. But I am going to do something else for you. It is not exactly what you asked me for. But you will see, in the end you will like it very much; you will find that all will go really well with you. Do you want a bet?'

With warmth and conviction he speaks about an important part of his life: 'I knew an amazing man. I have touched him with my hands so many times. My eyes were fixed on his face. The part of life I witnessed with him changed everything. On one wretched day I betrayed him, but he threw his arms around my neck to embrace me, and everything was forgotten by an experience that changes you within.

'I will tell you his story; I bet you will like it.'

Peter tells the story of Jesus to the lame man. Then, suddenly, the man ceases to listen and decides to try: he stands up straight. The story of Jesus which heals the lame has struck him. He wants to try it out for himself.

He stands on his own two feet. They are doing very well indeed. They support him when he tries to take two jumps and when he starts to run.

He is healed. The story which Peter has told him has restored him to life.

Peter really is a strange sort of person. He was asked for money and he said he had none. Fortunately he was penniless that day. The story of Jesus is worth more than all the money that he could give.

The lame man starts to run towards the Temple, shouting with joy. The power in his legs is transformed into his inner life: he has discovered Jesus the Lord.

The story does not finish here. The sequel is also important.

The man who was once lame causes such uproar within the Temple precincts that the chief priests are called and they seek to discover which devil is there. Peter's name comes up. They have an urgent meeting and they try him out of fear of public disorder. Someone implores him quite openly: 'Please, that's enough of this mania for healing the lame. If you continue you will come to the same end as your friend. We cannot allow it: for reasons of prudence.'

Peter replies in a haughty fashion: 'I cannot halt the desire for life which Jesus has entrusted to me. The man who was lame walked upright, just like a youngster of twenty, because everyone knows that he could not live – really live – unless it be in the name of Jesus of Nazareth. You have killed him, but God has raised him up for the life and hope of all. From now onwards I and my friends, the people of life, will proclaim him quite openly so that all may have life. And I really hope that you are not disappointed, we will do the same anyway.'

EDUCATION IN THE LAW

They had taken one of those rare moments of calm. Jesus was alone and in blessed peace after a day wholly spent in talking, replying, doing.

He was praying, immersed in contemplation of the Father. They came like madmen, dragging a poor, frightened and unkempt woman by the hair.

They threw her at his feet, like a sack of potatoes. 'She has been caught in adultery. There is no doubt about her guilt. Let's stone her to death. This is what the law prescribes, as you know only too well.' Jesus looked at them with amazement.

'You begin. Here's a stone: you throw it first. You have always spoken well about the law. Have courage, let us observe it together.'

That small group of teachers of the law were thinking that they had cornered him. Jesus had always spoken well of the law. He had asked for a precise and immediate observance. 'You cannot be permitted to change the written text: not even one full stop nor punctuation mark.' Now he had to choose: to keep the law and start throwing stones at the poor woman who had sinned, or to disown all his statements of principle and finally throw off the mask.

Jesus is silent. He continues to think and to pray as if nothing had happened. He does not like people who do things only because others have decided for them. They want to kill in the name of the law? They must see it themselves in their consciences and do not seek outside help.

The atmosphere is tense, heavy. Someone insists: 'Jesus, what now?' But Jesus waits in silence.

The law is important to him. But it is for life. It cannot become a principle of death. This is not the law that the Father has offered to humanity. This is how the powerful people of this world behave, who have little real interest in the lives of others.

Unnerved by Jesus' compassionate silence, those good Jews who wanted respect for the law at all costs found themselves immersed in death. They invoked the sin of that poor woman. And they were full of sin and death themselves.

They were now cornered. They were exposed and they took flight, they who knew only the woman's sin. They threw down the stones they already held in their hands and they fled.

One runs away in shame. Another goes away saved: he rediscovers the law, he who thought he knew it to perfection and wanted it applied to the letter.

Everyone had come there filled with death. They return home restored to life.

Finally, Jesus is alone. The poor woman is still on the ground, unable to raise her eyes from the dust in which she had been thrown.

Jesus bends down. He offers her his hand. He brings her to her feet: her head raised up, as he wishes. He peers into her eyes with a kindly look.

'You are alive. The law of life has saved you. You see how strange these things are? You were thinking you were alive because you had done what you wanted in spite of the law. And you were dead, even before you were condemned. Now you are alive: restored to life.

Now then, are you going to live like someone who is alive?'

'Yes, Jesus. Thank you. Can I remain with you?'

An important difference between us and the sinful woman's accusers deserves to be underlined.

Those people believed in the law. Perhaps we can discuss the type of fidelity and the interpretation they gave. But they believed in it.

We, however, live in an atmosphere of a deep and difficult crisis concerning the law. Often and quite willingly, we contest the law and the institutions which represent and uphold it. It is not a question of discovering which of the two is correct. The problem is quite different. Jesus firmly addresses it.

Institutions and the laws which regulate them have the duty of guiding us in love. But often they crush love. The law is unpredictable or weighted in favour of some people or groups. The institution becomes impersonal and obsessive and serves only to endorse the existing powers that be.

Unfortunately we pay the price of this every day: a ready distrust of the law, which unleashes a massive legal crisis. We must certainly find a solution.

The story of Jesus and the sinful woman warns us that the problem is not primarily one of method. It concerns the very substance of things.

Some want firm laws and strong punishments for transgressors. Sometimes even educational institutions settle for the same way of thinking. It seems eminently justified. In the end, everyone does this.

Jesus suggests a very special approach when dealing with the law. He counsels observance of laws down to the smallest details: a comma or punctuation mark unheeded is enough to result in something bad (Mt 5:17-19). And then, in the midst of life, even the most sacred laws are infringed: that of the Sabbath or that of the punishment of wrongdoers are designed to incur the wrath of his enemies (Jn 5:1-18).

In the end he is condemned to death as a transgressor

against the law, he who had pledged himself to its true observance, and who was against every form of legalism.

His life teaches us something serious and pressing: the perspective within which to think and plan with that daily labour which knows how to use knowledge and wisdom.

There is but one law: to give life where there is death, losing one's own life so that all may have life to the full.

This cries out as the result of that choice of life which brings about the confession that Jesus alone is Lord. The other laws – all of them, even if on different levels – are important. They often represent the necessary means of fostering life. Sometimes the demands of life are such as to force us to take the liberty of transgression. They are always so pressing as to counsel breaking the observance of the laws: truly, in the end, to sacrifice one's life.

LOOKING TO THE FUTURE

From time to time everyone likes to be able to part the veil of uncertainty which hangs over the future. In fact, to know in advance what will happen tomorrow gives security and power: whoever has some secret up his sleeve succeeds in making a good impression to his friends and thinks he has the answers to every type of problem.

Jesus' disciples were no exception. Now and again one of them, who was more curious than the others, even stirred things up with the hope of having a change of fortune: 'Go on, you are friends of Jesus, you have been with him for a while and he trusts you. Try to get details about what is going to happen. He says he has a direct link with God: he can surely reveal some secrets to you. It's enough to ask him in a proper manner.'

One day when things seemed more bleak than usual, the

disciples plucked up courage and asked him the question which had been worrying them for some time: 'Jesus, where are we going to?' Then, with a little impudence, they were more direct: 'Is it true that the end of the world is near? There are people around who are predicting it quite strongly. Are they reliable forecasts? When will this general overturning of things take place? Will there be any warning signs?'

In one breath they had asked Jesus everything they wanted to know. Now, they awaited his reply.

They had many reasons to ask this sort of question. When Jesus was speaking on these themes, he used to come down hard: 'You know about that poor man for whom the time had well and truly come. He had filled his house with produce of all kinds. The barns were no longer big enough: he hurriedly built new ones. Then, settling down to rest and to enjoy his wealth, he concluded: Now, finally, I can enjoy it in peace. Ah, for this poor man things did not really turn out like this: the day he made his great plans was the last day of his life. During the night death knocked at his door and drew him away.'

They insist: 'Of course, we must be prepared so as not to come to a bad end. But if one knows in advance what will happen, one can make better and more decisive preparations. So, Jesus, when? What signs will accompany the end of the world?'

Jesus does not evade the question. But he replies in his own way. Instead of putting forward signs and portents, he tells a story.

'Listen to me carefully. I will tell you a story. The details are not important. The substance is what matters, and then draw your own conclusion.

In our part of the world the night before a wedding is always the time for a bit of a feast. You are familiar with the customs and who knows how many times you yourselves have taken part in these kind of festivals.

The betrothed couple invite their closest friends. Singing,

dancing and eating, they prepare for the great event of the following day. As you know, the feast only begins when the groom joins the bride in her house.

Once upon a time ten young girls, friends of the bride, had been invited. They had the task of brightening up the feast both by their presence and with their lamps. Each one had thus brought with her a lamp and the necessary amount of oil. They had organised themselves even to the point of ensuring a good supply of oil so that they would not be stranded at the crucial moment.

Five bridesmaids were wise: they had brought plenty of oil in case the feast went on for a long time. However, the other five brought only what was strictly necessary.

Unfortunately, that night the groom was late. The five wise bridesmaids had a good stock of oil and were happy. The others, however, began to worry. They made a few rapid calculations and soon concluded that there wasn't enough oil. What a predicament, they thought, to be stranded at the crucial moment of the feast. They asked their friends for a little support: 'Please give us some of your oil.' The reply was firm and sharp: 'No. If we give some to you there will no longer be enough for us. Go and buy some. If you are quick you will get back in time for the beginning of the feast.'

It seems like good advice. But there is a problem: it's the middle of the night: there will surely not be any shop open at this hour.

They try everywhere, knocking on doors. Finally one opens. They replenish their oil stock and hurry back to the house where the feast is being held.

From far away they can hear the songs and the sound of dancing. They rush on. The door is closed: the feast is going on inside, outside it is dark and still. They persist. Someone opens up. They make to go in, pleading with the other five bridesmaids whose lamps were already filled with enough oil for the whole night. The reply is abrupt, like a slap in the face: 'No, no one knows you. There is nothing doing. Stay outside. The groom has already arrived and the feast is underway. You cannot come in. Go back home and don't waste any more of our time.'

That is the end of the story.

Jesus looks at the disciples. He wants to see whether anything had happened. They had a great question mark written all over their faces. They had asked him the date of the end of time and some warning sign, and Jesus replies by telling the strange story of five girls who ran out of oil owing to a lack of sense and foresight.

Jesus starts speaking again.

'Let's reflect together on the story I have told you.

Whoever replies to an invitation must make good use of his time and resources, so as not to end up in great difficulties at the crucial moment. This is the real plight of the five bridesmaids who had exhausted their supply of oil prematurely: if they had had a little more foresight, they would have come with a plentiful stock and no delay would have taken them by surprise.

You want to know when the end of the world will come knocking at the door of your life and of history – I cannot tell you because no one knows. This is God's great secret. But there is one thing that we know very well: the necessity of being people who are attentive, vigilant, having foresight. The end will come when no one expects it. It is like a thief: he empties the house if the owner is not careful. But the house of the man who is vigilant is always secure. No surprise can disturb him.'

'This much is clear: yet again, Jesus, you have unsettled us. Thank you'. The reply is heartfelt. 'But tell us, the girls who had brought their supply of oil with them, didn't they do well not to lend it? You have not let us know whose side you are on.'

Jesus replies quite clearly: 'The story is not to be read with the requirement of having to cast one's vote for all the characters. It is not said who is good and who is not. The groom had been late for his own reasons and the feast lasts longer than anticipated, because feasts cannot be controlled in that way.

The story offers something far more important: how we are to settle down to facing the future. The future is in God's hands. We must not seek to penetrate an unforeseeable mystery. Instead we must live in watchful expectation.

But we can anticipate the future: the solidarity which does not count the cost and throws all meanness to the wind, this anticipates the future for which we anxiously await.'

And he concludes: 'The five girls who had not wanted to share their oil with their friends, I do not have much sympathy with them. They have been quite selfish. I urge to imitate their vigilance and careful planning, certainly not the lack of fellowship and the fear of taking a risk.

To live in the present while anticipating the future requires us to do exactly the opposite: if someone asks you to go with them along the road one mile, go with him for four; if someone asks you to lend your cloak, give him your tunic as well; if you meet someone who is hungry, share your bread with him.'

WAYS OF SEEING THINGS

Every now and then David, like all of us, let himself go. This time, however, he had not really counted the cost.

Bathsheba had got into the naughty habit of taking a bath on the terrace. By dint of looking at her, David fell madly in love and was frantically seeking a way of carrying out his plan to seduce her.

He knew he had an image to protect and public duties to perform. He felt there was nothing for it but to give up Bathsheba. So he tried a little diplomacy.

From a distance he had found out about the marital situation of this beautiful lady. He discovered that Bathsheba's husband, a general in David's own army, was away from home, carrying out his military duties.

The idea gradually clarifies itself in David's mind. He cannot marry a woman who is already married. But he can marry a widow. It would even have created a good picture: he, the king, preferring a widow to thousands of easy proposals. 'What a good king we have' they would all say. And so he would gain Bathsheba and acclamation in the same stroke.

He has found a way. There is only one obstacle: Uriah, the husband of Bathsheba, is still alive and well, and fighting like a lion. He is alive, or rather, he *was* alive. With a little careful planning, he could become a war hero, the gold medal of military valour awarded to Bathsheba before the wedding feast as a memento of her husband who had fallen in battle.

King David gives some orders to his most trusted friends. 'Place Uriah at the centre of the battle, where the best-trained enemies are. Leave him on his own. Make it happen in the way all heroes die.'

Unfortunately they do as they are told, and Bathsheba finds herself with a medal but not a husband.

The period of mourning over, David makes a proposal of marriage. Solemn feasts take place and then everything is just as before. David is happy. Bathsheba is soon consoled. The people of Jerusalem speak well of their king's generosity. The future is very rosy.

The prophet Nathan is the only one not to be satisfied by what has happened. He does not go along with either the messy event nor its happy conclusion.

Having been well trained, he must denounce what has taken place and call upon David to change his life. What kind of prophet would he be if he kept silent? He feels he has a responsibility to intervene. But he cannot roar like a madman. To do so would not achieve anything. But above all – and what was worse – with no conversion in sight it ruled out that sowing of the seed by the troublesome prophet.

He asks for an audience. He is given one. He forces a smile as he speaks to David. 'David, they speak very well of you. I am happy because it is true. You are an excellent king. You love justice. You defend it, make sure it is honoured and you observe it yourself. You are a blessing from God upon your people.'

He has not said anything untrue. Bathsheba apart, David really was a near perfect king.

David listened to him with pleasure. He would even think: 'Nathan is a valuable and trustworthy man. He knows how to denounce and to praise. I must give him a little more consideration.'

'Listen, David, I want to tell you what is on my mind. I have been given evidence about something which has disturbed me. See if you can do something.' And he tells the story: 'I know a man who had one hundred sheep. One day a friend went to meet him. They talked at length because it had been months since they had seen one another. The man who owned the hundred sheep invited his friend to stay with him for lunch. He promised him an excellent meal of roast lamb. Everything is all right so far, but what follows disturbs me.

Think about it, David. He had one hundred sheep. To share a feast with his friend, but he had taken the sheep from a neighbour. That poor man had only one sheep. He used to care for it like a son. And he who had one hundred sheep stole it to feast with his friend.'

David grew red in the face: 'He did such a disgraceful thing? Is it possible? Are you sure? His sin is very serious indeed. That man deserves to die. Nathan, tell me his name. I'll see to it. Straight away.'

Nathan looked at him in silence. David is perturbed. The injustice committed has sent him into a rage. 'Nathan, the name! That man is going to be punished, immediately and without mercy.'

Nathan still looks at David. Then, decidedly, he breaks the silence: 'David, you are the man.'

David shivers. In his zeal he had taken out his sword and was brandishing it as if he had a band of enemies in front of him. He put it back in its sheath, sad and disconsolate. 'It's true, that man is me, because I have done this. I, the anointed of the Lord. Nathan, thank you. Help me to put things right.'

Probably, with the same fury with which he had been waving the sword a few moments before, he took the lyre in his hands and sung the following lament: 'Have mercy on me, Lord. I have sinned against you. Blot out my sin.'

And what if Nathan's way was to make suggestions at a time of unseemly shouting and resigned silence?

ENOUGH OF MATERIALISM

One day a young man came up to Jesus. He was a good fellow, serious. He had developed his question while carefully preparing for the meeting. Unfortunately, the old way of thinking, rooted in the religious experience of his people, surfaced even at such a decisive time in his life. 'Jesus, what will it cost me to have eternal life? Give me a suggestion and I pledge myself to accepting it.' Jesus responds pointedly, as he usually did. He wants to educate the young man, leading him from observance of the law to the freedom of love.

'Keep the commandments.' 'Jesus, I have kept them since I was very young. Those who know me can vouch for that. I feel at peace, but it's not enough. This is why I came looking for you. What more must I do?' Jesus smiled at him with great warmth. He really was a fine young man. He changes his tone: 'It's true: you are a fine fellow. You are capable of a great leap forward. Stop drawing up accounts with God and your conscience. Throw yourself on the generosity of love.' 'What must I do': he continues thinking in terms of a contract between two parties. Jesus tells tall stories. He wants to make out that there is not a fair price. Love is beyond price: foolish and generous at the same time.

'This is my proposal: sell everything and come with me. There is nothing to be gained. It is not true that if you follow me you will have a hundred times more than what you gave up. Everyone would have done so. I do not know what is to be earned. But I do know that we can restore life and hope to all. Come with me. Have courage, leave everything and come with me.'

That young man was good and generous. But he had one big fault: he was afraid to take risks. So he had said no to Jesus, so he didn't have to take a risk. He went away sad and dejected. If Jesus had asked him for a high price, he could have stayed. He knew that God is demanding and exacts a very high price. And he would have dared to pay it. But Jesus asks him to make an act of gratuitous love, just like God's love. He cannot take the risk: it is beyond what he had bargained for.

Jesus is patient when faced with a young man trained in the rabbinical schools. But he did not really want to be the same with his own disciples, whom he had chosen and trained himself.

But alas, even they were thinking in the same terms of 'how much will it cost me' and 'what will we gain.'

They spoke about it among themselves. They had reflected on Jesus' words when he had called them from their homes and their work, to see if, at least implicitly, there was some form of compensation to be had.

They had not remembered anything important. Jesus' remarks were from a completely different perspective.

They pluck up courage and address the very nub of the question. 'Listen, Jesus', begins Peter, who was responsible for opening the conversation on this burning issue, 'you must be clear about it. All the teachers do this when dealing with their disciples. We have left everything to follow you. We are faithful to you. But now it is time to take stock. What gain is there for us?' It is out in the open, a little painful and with a hint of shame. But they could do no more. When he had first spoken, the others had echoed his words, 'Jesus, what do we gain by remaining with you?' They were hoping for a greater reward. They had even exaggerated the list of things that they had given up to follow Jesus. They wanted him to be moved, pushing him to raise the reward.

As usual, Jesus replies in successive waves.

Already the first blow had struck hard. He had hoped it would have been sufficient. And yet...

'Listen carefully because this is a serious matter. You have left brothers, sisters, mothers and fathers to be with me. Of course I promise you a reward one hundredfold. But make no mistake, my disciple must be ready to hate father, mother, brothers and sisters to serve the Gospel. And houses: are one hundred enough for you? I have not a single stone where I can put my head at night. I promise you the same thing. The Kingdom demands everything of you. This is why whoever follows me will have trials and sufferings when proclaiming the Gospel.

But one thing is certain: you will have a special place in the Father's house.'

Jesus' reply wasn't really much consolation to them in terms of the 'what's in it for us' and 'what will it cost me' mentality.

He returns to his task. By now they wanted to return to the heart of the matter. We must thank these obstinate and unperceptive friends of Jesus. They have given us the heart and mind of Jesus on such an important question.

'Aim for eternal life. There at least we will have a special place: the first places, at the right and the left... Those who were laughing at us behind our backs must then take notice.' They do their calculations and make their arrangements: a place for you and one for me. It is not easy to make such a division. They dispute among themselves and even their mothers intervene in the hope of influencing Jesus.

It's always the same question: we have left everything – what will we gain, at least in eternal life?

Jesus can stand it no longer. A place in the Father's house is not like a seat in the stadium. One does not but the ticket, at any price. Neither less nor more money is needed, and there are no first or second places. Here, in the Father's house, the logic of love rules. The Father opens his house because he loves his children. He throws open the doors to everyone, in a love which has the initiative and which welcomes all in the same fashion. The Father's love is so great and unexpected that even if our hearts reproach us for something (and woe to him who does not allow his heart to reproach him), God is greater than our heart.

Jesus ends by saying 'Do you wish to know everything?' 'If signs must be given, these are for the poor, the sinners, and the very least, even the prostitutes. The last are first in my Father's house.'

WHO IS THE HUMAN PERSON?

Jesus' disciples had never asked him: who or what is the human person?

Their doubts were about God. Jesus himself had raised them, when he had started preaching certain things about God, things so different from those which came from the mouths of the doctors of the law.

Jesus had said some very beautiful things about God. It pleased his disciples. Life and hope were restored, even when there were thousands of reasons for being despondent.

Now and again they asked: Who will be right, Jesus or the doctors of the law? Little by little, the hope that Jesus would be right was becoming a certainty.

But they did not have any doubts about human beings. For them what they knew was all right. But Jesus was really concerned about this. They had not yet perceived that the way in which he was presenting God contrasted with the image of humanity that they acknowledged.

For the disciples, who were reasoning according to the cultural models of the time, there were important people and those who were worth little or nothing. Jesus pleased them when he was invited to a meal by the prominent people of the area. But they couldn't bear it when he stopped on the road to speak with sinners, lepers and even prostitutes.

The disciples were convinced that it would have been easy to distinguish between good and bad people: it was enough to apply the law. Instead Jesus was saying that the first places in the kingdom of heaven are reserved to those who counted the least. One day he had even come to say that the shepherd must run after the wayward sheep, leaving the ninety-nine on their own. They had received a severe rebuke when they decided to lend a hand to the fishermen to divide the good fish from the bad. They had understood him perfectly: the question was not to do with fish, but with human beings. Jesus had not sent them to say: only God knows who is good and who is evil and he does not reveal this to anyone.

The day came when the poor disciples could stand it no longer. They had taken their master to one side and had asked him in no uncertain terms: 'Tell us whose side you are on'. Then straight away, and more decisively: 'You must tell us which kind of people please you, because we are so confused it frightens us.'

They were hoping for definitions and lists. Someone was ready to note the reply.

Jesus chooses another approach: 'I am going to tell you

a story. Listen carefully and try to discover what lies beneath it.' He replies like this to the question about the human person, first of all making them see the way in which we must seek a response when in the midst a great mystery.

'One day two men went to pray at the temple. Two more different types cannot be imagined. One was a fine, zealous Pharisee, known to all for his observance of the law. The other was a tax collector: a bad sort, who had robbed others of their money without any scruples. It was surprising that he had gone to pray.

The Pharisee took the place of honour. Standing up, his head held high, he repeated the prayer he said every day: 'I thank you, God. You have been kind and generous to me and I have repaid you in the same way. We are equal: I can look you in the face, as I look at those who are the same as me. I pay the tithes, I make the prescribed offerings, I keep all the laws. I am good, thanks to God and my own diligence.'

Then he finishes by saying: 'I have no more need of you. From now on I'll do it on my own. Spare your thanks. What I save, I can give to that poor man down there. Do you see how generous I am? Thank you, my God.' That is the end of the Pharisee's prayer.

The wretched tax collector, hidden below behind a column, was also trying to pray. It was so awful, because he was in a crisis and prayer in a crisis greatly disgusted him. It is difficult to think about oneself to think about one's own life before God is a tragedy... at least not to be good like that Pharisee up there.

Jesus reports some of the words used by the tax collector as he prayed: "Lord, have mercy on me for I am a poor sinner, up to my neck in difficulties. You know how much it costs me to pray to you. Every time I think about you in prayer, I discover more about who I am, I count the betrayals that mark my life, I compare your merciful goodness with my life. My accounts do not balance and the crisis deepens.

You know, sometimes I have the wish to abandon this

prayer. So I would be able to see it myself alone. And finally I would be able to please myself and my crisis would end. Perhaps. But that is no good. It is not right. And then I am sure that I will not achieve it. Without you, I am dead.

I ask two things of you. They are very important to me. I know I do not deserve them. But I'm asking you all the same.

First of all, I ask you the grace to continue to come here to pray, in spite of everything. I have found that it is very good to contemplate you, even if it hurts me. In your face, I see my own. I cry out to you from the depths. Make me well. Help me to live. To pray is like dreaming in colour about one's own life: I do not really want to lose even the privilege of dreaming.

This is the second thing, and it is more difficult. It depends on you alone. I am not so good at saying it! Read between the lines. Here goes: I am trying to tell you what I want. Take me as I am. Welcome me into your arms, poor devil that I am. I cannot live without you. I really cannot do it. You must not ask me to be good as the condition of your love. I will remain alone, sad, desperate. Give me your all-embracing love and you will see that, bit by bit, something will change in my life."

That is the end of the story.

The disciples remained silent and amazed. They had been seeking a definition of a good and fulfilled person. The story told by Jesus had confounded them. Yet again Jesus had overdone it. They were used to hearing and taking advice: duty, good will, the task of setting things in motion. Jesus takes the opposite stance: he asks for the ability to become involved in a crisis and the willingness to entrust oneself to God. This is why he does not get on well with the pharisees. It is almost as if he is on the side of the tax collector.

They ask him: 'Jesus, whose side are you on?'

They didn't have to wait for a reply: 'My tenderness

towards sinners knows no bounds. I am ready to embrace them, as a father throws his arms around the neck of the boy who ran away from home.' The disciples look at him: 'Which boy?' 'Do you not know the story of the boy who was given money by his father and wasted everything he had, and then returned home in a state of desperation? One of these days I will tell you that story.'

God welcomes sinners who raise their arms towards him. He pardons them and fills them with his love. He loves us first. He does not ask for conditions. He loves us and that is enough. All the rest follows, as the fruit of his love.

Jesus finishes what he is saying: 'Is it now clear who the human person is? How many false ideas you must still change.'

WHOSE SIDE ARE YOU ON, GOD?

It seemed a strange case, but it happened to Jesus every Sabbath. One Sabbath, in fact, Jesus was speaking in the synagogue as was his custom, when the official handed him the scroll. He was speaking about God in a special way. Everyone had become aware that he had very beautiful and original experiences to which he made reference. It very nearly became automatic to think that he had seen him and knew some special secret about him.

But he was not doing it to gain influence. Moreover, the temptation never entered his head to use this first hand information to put on airs or place himself a step higher than his listeners. It was not for nothing that he was acting like the doctors of the law who usually commented on the Scriptures at the Sabbath meetings. On the contrary, he talked like everyone else: without fine-sounding words and with cross-references and comparisons, full of the flavour of everyday life.

In a word, it was a pleasure to listen to him when he was speaking about God.

At that very moment the back door of the synagogue creaked as if someone had tried to peep inside.

Few had worried about it: an unexpected gust of wind or some curious person who, having arrived late, sought not to be noticed.

Jesus stops. He calls Peter. One of the few people who had noticed the small commotion thinks: 'It is sent to rebuke that nuisance who has disturbed such a serious meeting. It serves him right. At least at the Sabbath meetings it would be as well to learn to be on time.'

Jesus had very different plans: 'Listen, Peter, tell that poor woman outside the door not to be afraid. Tell her to come forward. I want to give her a gift she has not even dreamed of.'

'Who knows how he had become aware of her? This Jesus has a thousand eyes and misses nothing.' Poor Peter had still not discovered that love has an eye which can even see through walls.

The woman comes forward. She goes to the middle of the room, full of shame. Everyone looks at her. She is seriously ill. It is a very bad form of arthritis that has almost bent her double. She walks with a stoop, her gaze fixed on the ground.

She waits. Everyone waits, including those three people at the back of the room with an inquisitive attitude of one who has no interest in what is being said, but survey everything in order to report back to whomsoever.

Jesus turns to the woman crippled with arthritis and looks at her in a way that speaks more than thousands of words. His eyes burn with the will to heal her. The things he had been saying about God had finally come about.

Peter is worried. He has a responsibility to Jesus and the group of disciples. He steps in before Jesus puts them all in difficulties. 'Jesus, do not heal her. Today is the Sabbath. If you do it they will accuse us of breaking a sacred law.

Already the chief priests and doctors of the law cannot see us because of the things you are saying about God. If you start breaking another law we've had it. Please, Jesus, a little sense does not go amiss.'

Jesus did not hear. Peter's way of thinking does not go down well with him. He is thinking of that poor woman who is sick; he thinks of what he was saying about God. He seems to have reached a conclusion: enough talking, they want action, otherwise they will continue to turn away from God. This cannot go on. God makes human life his greatest joy and these people are reducing him to a policeman who controls everything, ready to dish out fines and punishments. There is even the risk that someone will think that God is happy to see people suffer.

He wants to be quite clear. He does not like the statements they are making. He takes the bull by the horns.

Jesus addresses the head of the synagogue and the three doctors of the law who were there to oversee things. 'Aren't there seven of you doctors of the law? Well, you know everything about God. You explain things about him to others with great confidence. It almost seems as if God had entrusted his secrets to you. Now then, please tell me this: if I, for example, were to heal this poor woman today, on the Sabbath, would God be happy? In your opinion, which side is he on? What is his will? In your opinion, and you know all about him, is it more fitting to heal a sick person or to observe the Sabbath?'

Jesus is not kind. He presents hard choices: where does God stand in this specific situation. Healing or law? They are not to take refuge in the easiest solution: both are important things, each in its own place. They must choose.

The reply comes quickly: 'Jesus, keep the law and do not allow yourself to do what is forbidden. The law is the law. Heal her tomorrow. She has waited for eighteen years. She can wait another day.'

Faced with this form of reasoning, which betrays a very narrow idea of God, Jesus loses his patience, just like the day when he overturned the moneylenders' stalls in the entrance to the Temple. This is God's work, his plan for human life, his mystery of love. If he lets it be lost, he will be betraying it forever.

We must be forever grateful to him. For a few moments he has opened God's heart to us.

Again he addresses the three doctors of the law, the head of the synagogue who was of the same mind as them, and all those who believed they knew about God. 'You say that you are children of the God of Abraham, Isaac and Jacob. You say that when your enemies in Egypt forced you to walk with heads bowed down, under the weight of the boulders they placed upon your shoulders, God intervened directly, he set you free from slavery. He made you a people who walked with heads held high. You do well to say that this is really true. But there is only one problem. In the name of this God who made you walk upright you want me to leave this poor woman bent double for one more day? You are wrong. You have not really understood anything about God. God is happy when people walk upright.'

He returns to the sick woman: 'Lift up your head. You are healed. You are alive. At last you can see everything in front of you.' Then he speaks to the crowd, who were happy and amazed at what had happened: 'Have you understood who God is and on whose side he is? First I told you in words but now I say it with actions and I am much happier. Actions speak much louder than words.'

Peter's fears were justified. This time Jesus has really done it. They decide to kill him. They drag him to the edge of the precipice on which the city is built and seek to throw him down, as was done with blasphemers. This time Jesus slips through their hands. But then, a few months later, he freely gives himself up to death, to have the last word about the mystery of God.

SELF-GIVING LOVE

Jesus was used to being bombarded with questions. He provoked many of them himself, with his own unusual way of doing things. Some questions voiced the desire of the thirsty who run towards a spring of water. Some arose from the wish to see things more clearly, or even from a tinge of curiosity about this man who had come from a region which had never produced anything good.

The doctor of the law who came up to Jesus that day did not fall into any of these categories. His question was a type of examination. This 'teacher of the law' felt obliged to check Jesus' orthodoxy in order to give an informed opinion.

He had put the obligatory question: 'Jesus, tell me... what must I do to have eternal life?' The question was too easy for a religious man but a problem for one who seldom went to the Temple or read the Scriptures. From the reply it was straight away possible to give a judgement on Jesus' competence and sincerity.

Jesus did not send him to hell as perhaps we might have done, angered by his provocative attitude. He did not even submit him to judgement. With a disarming smile he says: 'Why do you ask me? You are the doctor of the law. You know these things better than I do.'

The response is not long in coming. The doctor of the law displays his theological learning: 'Two things are necessary to have eternal life: to love God and to love one's neighbour. This is the law that Moses taught us.'

Now Jesus takes on the role of the examiner. He gives him full marks. 'Perfect. The title you have, you really do merit it. I advise one thing: put into practice what you know so well.' He takes the first step to get away. The interrogation is over.

The doctor of the law does not make do with this. He really can't accept the very bad image created. So he resumes his discourse with a new question.

This time he is particularly careful. He does not want to fall into a fresh trap. He gets into difficulties: 'Tell me, Jesus, who is my neighbour, whom I must love as I love God?' He does not ask about God. He is afraid that Jesus will say to him: 'How come you ask me? You are the doctor of the law. Every day you explain to the people what God's will is in everything. Please, do not make me waste any more time.'

About one's neighbour, however, even a doctor of the law can have his doubts. The law and traditions were clear enough in identifying who was the neighbour to be loved: based on occupation, place of birth, family pedigree and certain illnesses, but the specific interpretations varied. This is why the doctor of the law can address such an intelligent question to Jesus. It is the perfect opportunity to weigh up Jesus' theological position and even answer some unresolved questions.

'Who is my neighbour?' He asks for a type of list. He imagines that Jesus will say to him: so-and-so and so-and-so are 'neighbours' for a good Jew who keeps the law. The others are not.

He too, like so many, is a prisoner of the 'addressees' trap, those for whom he has a preferential love, and he is looking for a list divided into two columns: those who are one's neighbour and those who are not, with some names placed half way. Instead Jesus replies by telling a story.

'One day a man who was going down from Jerusalem to Jericho was attacked by a band of robbers. They took everything and then left him on the path, more dead than alive.

He was in desperate need of help. Thirst burned his throat. What little strength he had was spent. He could do no more. But travellers were very rare in those parts. Next to no one passed by on that day.'

Having set the scene, Jesus joins his hands. Three characters are going to pass by. He chooses them with care. They are symbolic figures, quite unequivocal: the 'good', being precisely those who are officially good and honest; and the 'bad', with none so bad as them.

'A priest passes by, taken up with his worries and concerns. He does not take any notice of the poor man lying at the side of the path. He continues on his way. A little while later a Levite also passes along the same path. Not even he is bothered and he carries on. He has many pastoral duties and he doesn't really have the time to attend to this.

Finally, a Samaritan comes that way. Immediately he notices the desperate situation of the poor man who had run into the band of robbers.

He stops. He is in no doubt: at this moment the only important thing to do is to lend a hand to someone who is suffering.

He gets down from his horse. He gives the man something to drink. He does his best to treat the man's wounds. He puts him in the saddle and makes straight for Jericho, trying to find a doctor. He finds one. The treatment is completed. Then he takes him to an inn and entrusts him to the care of the innkeeper. He tenders a generous sum of money to pay for any immediate needs and promises to pay the balance on his return.'

Jesus looks at the doctor of the law. He is a little uneasy. Jesus must have saved up this gallery of characters. He knows that there is bad blood between Jews and Samaritans. He has made the priest and Levite out to be bad, but makes a Samaritan out to be good and generous – this is too much.

Jesus has not forgotten the question which gave rise to the story. The doctor of the law had wanted to know 'Who is my neighbour?' He was ready to take note: a list of those to be loved and concerned about and, most probably, a page for those whom he should let well alone.

He wanted a list. With such a useful sheet in his hands he could easily find his bearings with regard to whom he was dealing with (in his love for others and his religious duties). In disputed cases it was enough to quote Jesus and everything would be settled.

Jesus did not give any list to the doctor of the law, nor even to us. On the contrary, he turns that way of thinking on its head.

Who one's 'neighbour' is cannot be anticipated or programmed to fit in with decisions or by recourse to tradition. Whoever has need of me and calls upon me, he or she is my neighbour, whom I must love and serve. The question is not about other people, who may or may not be on the list of those to be concerned with. It does not even refer to a definite style of service nor a type of response in which we can be specialists.

The question is about you and me: the human family and the community of the Church. We must become capable of 'being neighbours' to whomsoever is in need.

'Have you understood?', Jesus asks the doctor of the law. 'Well, now go and do the same thing. Is that clear?'

A SIGNIFICANT EXPERIENCE

'Let's speak plainly; it is well nigh time to take stock of our experience': suddenly Jesus addressed his disciples in a rather different tone than usual. They looked at him bewildered and amazed. They thought: 'What is happening? What does Jesus want today?'

Jesus replies in a forthright manner: 'Who do you say I am?' Everyone was aware that the question concealed another, more challenging one: 'Why are you with me?'

They had not really expected such a provocative question. They reply with excuses, in the hope of changing the discussion. Someone says: 'Jesus, the people have great admiration for you. Surely you have noticed it very often. They maintain that you are a prophet, like those in times past, even that you are the best among all of them. The people also use names: they call you Moses, Elijah. They still have a great nostalgia for John, who baptised on the banks of the Jordan and spared no one with his fiery words, and they are sure that you are like him. You are the greatest of the prophets.' They are ready to continue. They are pleased with themselves because the extended litany of praise puts off the nightmare of having to give a personal reply. Jesus interrupts them: 'I know. But what I am concerned about is you: you have been with me for so many months now, who do you say I am?

A long drawn-out silence descends. Perhaps they haven't thought about it for long enough. Too many factors encroach upon their decision and they are afraid of coming out with them in public.

Peter breaks the silence: 'Jesus, I will tell you who you are for us.' Well done, Peter, if it were not you, we would have to invent you'. The disciples began to smile. 'Tell me, Peter, who do you say I am?' Peter replies, borne along by the same enthusiasm with which, some months before, he had welcomed Jesus' call: 'You are the Messiah. We have waited and hoped for you, like one who thirsts searching for a spring of fresh water. You are God's gift to us, the sign of his love and his Covenant.' It was a textbook response; the disciples applaud. Everyone declares: 'We agree with Peter. For us Jesus is the Christ.'

Now they truly hope that Jesus will change the subject. These questions, which penetrate the very depths of human existence, always unsettle them a little.

Jesus is happy with Peter's reply. But it is not enough. He is afraid that it is a response which, although given with conviction and knowledge, is still too external. We give many replies like this and they do not cost too much, because they come quickly and directly from the stock of phrases uttered for good effect.

This time he takes the initiative by expressions which leave no room for uncertainty: 'Do not say in a roundabout way that I am the Messiah. Each of you must discover it for yourself. And then the time is still not right. Too many prejudices impair the image of God's Messiah.

Let us go back to ourselves: as friends we can share the most intense experiences. Listen to me carefully: I want to tell you a secret. Whoever speaks about God too freely comes up against a lot of mistaken ideas. Too many people think they know all about God and judge what I do and say by their own theological ideas. I am a nuisance to them. They are plotting to kill me.

It seems strange to your way of thinking: what I signify in God's plan is truly here, in my decision to offer my whole life for those whom God loves. The prophets of old spoke about it, but few people listened to them. This is being fulfilled in me: I am to be taken prisoner, condemned and put to death. God, who is my Father and yours, will raise me to life.' Then he adds: 'If you do not believe, wait a little while and you will see how events will prove me right. I assure you it is true, but do not be afraid.'

Peter and the others were breathless. 'It is not possible. You do only good to people. Who wants to kill you?' Peter replies, decisive as ever: 'You cannot submit yourself to this. Resist, Jesus, you must call us and we will defend you.'

Jesus looks at Peter with great sadness: 'Peter, you have understood nothing. First you spoke about important matters. But you are aware that they were empty words. Life is born out of death, I have told you this so many times. I give up my life: this is the way in which I declare that I am the Messiah of God, this is God's plan for everyone's life. Peter, you speak like Satan. Get away from me.'

Now, at last, everything is clear: to be with Jesus involves no little risk. One who speaks as he does is frightening. He seems like a hot-headed fanatic. If he is to meet a bad end, then surely not even his enemies will be saved. Is it worthwhile? Isn't it better to go back while there is still time? Disquiet creeps among the disciples. Someone mutters under his breath what others too were thinking: 'He does not have any sense. He is taking us to the brink. It is better to let him go on his way. We too are familiar with the Scriptures and we know whose side God is on.'

Peter was the worst. His declaration had been sincere; but even more sincere was his concern that Jesus should meet with tragedy. To be reprimanded by Jesus, to be made out to be a demon, this was too much.

Jesus does not force the issue. He reads the look on his disciples' faces and finds them discouraged and dejected. It's very bad indeed. They are his friends, those to whom he has entrusted his secrets and his great desire. He cannot abandon them to such discouragement and it is certainly not the time to continue discussing things with them. By now the relationship is beginning to disintegrate and words are not enough to mend the tear. Yet he cannot retract anything he has said. In this case as well, being confronted with the truth is one of the most educational experiences possible.

He plans an alternative solution, one of those capable of enkindling hope and trust even from the ashes of the deepest crises.

He calls Peter and two more of the most influential ones. He draws them against their will. 'Where are we going?' 'Have faith, come with me.' Then he says to the other disciples: 'Wait for us here: we will return soon and continue our conversation.'

In silence, after a long trek, they start to climb the side of the mountain. They do not ask for explanations. They follow him, just as they have done on so many other occasions, with that glimmer of hope which is never really driven from their hearts, despite everything.

Quite out of breath, they finally reach the summit. Jesus invites them to rest awhile and he moves a little away from them.

All of a sudden a dazzling light pierces the brightness of a sunny day. Peter and his friends turn round. They see Jesus in a whirl of blinding light. His clothes have become white. With him, emerging from the mystery, they catch sight of the prophets Moses and Elijah. They are speaking with Jesus. There is no doubt about it: that really is Jesus. His face, his appearance, the splendour with which he is surrounded, this is quite new. It is something the disciples have never seen before.

Peter breaks the silence: 'Jesus, are we dreaming? What we know see is a foretaste of that place about which you have so often spoken. This is your house. You have left it to pitch your tent in our midst. Let us remain here. I will make three tents: one for you, one for Moses and one for Elijah. Don't worry about us. The joy we experience when we are with you is sufficient. It is enough for us to contemplate you. Jesus, stay here forever.' The words left his mouth like a river in full flood. This time he was utterly sincere.

A hand touched his shoulder. 'Peter, let's go down. We cannot remain here on the mountain: the task which the Father has given me urges me on. I must go forward. I cannot stop. Too many people are still covered by the shadow of death. Quickly, let's go down.'

Jesus has returned to normal. His clothes are those woven by his mother; his face shines with the smile with which those who met him were used to seeing. The two figures he had been speaking to had also disappeared.

They resume their journey: from the mountain towards the group of tiny houses in which the other disciples were waiting for them.

The return is a happy one. Jesus speaks calmly, in the same warm tone as usual.

'Look, Peter – and John and James this goes for you as well, it goes for all of you. We have had a new and unexpected experience. I have touched you with something of the mystery of my own existence. When I spoke about my death, you were thrown into confusion – you even doubted me. You took me for a fanatic or someone deluded who goes clutching at straws.

You have come to your senses, without a doubt. Death reveals the meaning of life. You were thinking in terms of a powerful and triumphant Messiah. The prospect of my death has destroyed this image. You have come to the conclusion that perhaps I am not the Messiah.

I am not the sign from God whom you imagine. I have said to you so many times: God my Father shows his power in love, and there is no one who loves more than the one who is ready to give his or her own life for those whom they love. My death is the sign of a love far greater than you can ever imagine.

I am the Christ of God. Try hard to believe it. I have given you a little proof, a glimpse of God's glory to strengthen your hope.'

'Jesus, excuse us. We are your way of thinking. Trust us. We are pleased – you will see that in a little while you will be pleased with us.' They also think about the demand to stop the world to remain forever on the mountain to contemplate the splendour of Jesus' transfiguration. They are aware that it was a powerful temptation. 'Jesus, we also beg pardon for the foolish desire to stay on the mountain. It was certainly a joyful moment, but you are right: we must return to daily life. We place our trust in you and our hope in your plan.'

Jesus finishes by saying: 'You are forgiven. They are things which happen to everyone: it is normal to want to continue a beautiful experience. But it is a dangerous temptation. Every so often one must strengthen one's hope, but then one must courageously return to one's daily life.'

Peter, James and John are once again with the other disciples. 'What happened?': they ask this with eyes full of curiosity. 'Jesus has given us a wonderful experience, and now he has helped us to discover its meaning.'

Peter felt himself endowed with great responsibility: 'Sit down. Now I am going to tell you about the experience we have had, but above all I want to convey the message it brings. The experience is a gift of Jesus to three of us. It is not clear why he chose us three. But the message is what counts the most: this is a gift for everyone: for you and for those who will believe through your words.'

WISHING TO SEE JESUS

Jesus was one of those fine people before whom no one succeeded in remaining indifferent. He aroused enthusiasm or he made one angry.

So many people sought him out, for the strangest reasons. He was sought by those who were waiting for him to heal them, give them good word, or at the very least a smile so that they could continue to hope. With the same determination others tried to get rid of him, with the excuse that he was dangerous because he upset the formal observance of the law. Now and again his relatives and friends had also had to go and look for him: all of a sudden he used to disappear and no one knew where he had ended up.

His life had started with the theme of searching. To bring him into the world Mary and Joseph had had to find a quiet corner, because for this poor family there was no room anywhere. The shepherds, the magi, Herod: they had all looked for him. Even the very last moments of his earthly life had been marked by searching: he had been sought by the one who wanted to arrest him and to make no mistake about it; those who wanted to see him for the last time went to look for him in the tomb.

His disciples had often been tempted to inject a little order into the anxious searching after Jesus. They laid down a timetable to allow him a few hours of sleep. They had selected those who had the right to see him from those who were simply a nuisance. For this reason they wanted to exclude children, those who were noisy and confused, and sinners, who were too much of a threat to his dignity. The poor things, they did it to protect Jesus' very being, which was besieged from all sides. They wanted to arrange things as they were usually done: to distinguish between legitimate demands and those that were spurious, those that were serious and those made from mere curiosity.

Jesus had never been like that. He did not fit into their plans. Whoever loves and desires life certainly cannot make a list of priorities nor decide beforehand who is genuinely seeking him or who is making fun of him.

Many people looked for Jesus. One story, however, is more engaging than the others, the story of Zacchaeus.

Zacchaeus was not much good. Everyone knew it and told him to his face, with a modicum of reserve only because he was a powerful man and with powerful people it is better to tread carefully. He too knew this very well, but it was not that important to him. He had a lot of money, and with money one resolved every problem.

His troubles were precisely those of money. Many were envious of it; a lot of people contested the way he came by it. Zacchaeus was a tax collector, one of those who exacted money mercilessly, to right and left, on behalf of the Romans. He gave some money to them; some he kept himself. And so he had a stack of money and enemies. The good Jews, as attached to money as everyone else, and being frustrated nationalists, had not really forgiven him for this.

He was living in Jericho, a very beautiful city, which despite being in the desert had plenty of water, its air scented with roses.

One day he gets to know that Jesus was to pass through his city. He is curious. Straightaway he decides, 'I must see him; they talk about him a lot; unless I take advantage of it now, I will miss it forever.' He speaks about it with his friends. They tease him: 'Zacchaeus, have you decided to be converted? Is your money no longer enough for you? Think what your enemies will say. Don't give them the satisfaction.' Zacchaeus had made up his mind: 'There is no danger of that. I want to see him, and that's it. I have sympathy with that group of fishermen who follow him.' Someone whispers to him: 'Zacchaeus, be careful. Jesus is a dangerous sort. He sends word to no one.' 'For goodness sake, keep calm! I am used to it. I will let him speak, as I do with everyone. And then I will introduce myself. I have the money, not him, who is starved to death and has nowhere to live.'

Zacchaeus gets ready to see Jesus. He considers the different possibilities. He dismisses as too easy a solution that of persuading Jesus with a gift of alms at the right moment, in order to make him pass by the window of his house. He prefers to go out on to road himself.

But there is a problem. Zacchaeus has a small physical defect: he is very short in stature. Now he notices it. If he mixes with the crowd, he can say goodbye to catching sight of Jesus. He would not be able to see anything; the more so since Jericho is full of fanatics who have been on the streets since the night before, in order not to miss the slightest bit of the spectacle of Jesus passing by.

Zacchaeus thinks about it. He asks for advice. Then he makes up his own mind: 'I will climb a tree, in spite of my dignity.'

He also goes out by night, so as not to be seen. He settles down to rest in his tree until Jesus comes by. 'I wish to see him.'

At last Jesus passes by. Zacchaeus holds his breath. This is the most difficult moment. If someone notices him, pity his dignity and say goodbye to his brazenness. Tomorrow, in the tax office, everyone will look at him and mock him from head to foot.

Here's Jesus. Ah, what's happening? Is he stopping? He stops right under Zacchaeus' tree. He gets down from his mount and looks up. 'Zacchaeus.' Zacchaeus trembles with shame. 'Zacchaeus, come down, I must speak with you.' At last it was done. Zacchaeus gets down and stands in front of Jesus, ready for anything.

Jesus smiles at him. Smiles at Zacchaeus? Then he speaks. He doesn't reprimand him, not even a word of advice. Jesus says: 'Zacchaeus, I have decided: today I am coming to have a meal in your house. Are you coming?'

Zacchaeus feels his heart throbbing. He had wanted to see Jesus out of curiosity, not to be left out when his friends were speaking about him. And now Jesus upsets all his plans. He proposes to come as a guest into his house and his life.

Zacchaeus does not think twice. He replies willingly, with overflowing joy. 'Jesus, thank you. Come. I'm getting ready in a hurry. We will have a meal to remember.'

Jesus placed his arm around Zacchaeus' shoulders. He has neither reprimanded him nor imposed any other condition. He has restored his full dignity. He has reconciled him to himself: the first person after years of rebukes, which had been wearisome as much as useless. He can welcome Jesus as a guest to his house: if Jesus has said so, it is a sign that he can do it. Zacchaeus rediscovers the joy of being in harmony with himself.

But Jesus' embrace throws everything to the wind. It unsettles and it challenges. 'Unless I change my life', Zacchaeus thinks, 'what has Jesus come to do in my house?' He throws himself into the enthusiasm of conversion. Life changes in that intense moment so that only love and forgiveness know how to flourish: 'I am going to restore what I have stolen four times over. I am going to give my money to the poor, and share my life with them. From today, I change everything.'

Someone murmurs. He no longer understands. Where will all this end? That man Jesus is really dangerous. The bad are becoming good. Zacchaeus' wish to see Jesus was not 'good'. Jesus should have rebuked him and that would have been enough. This way of carrying on is too submissive.

Now Jesus steps in. He cannot have anything more to do with this mania for judging, separating and evaluating before welcoming.

He raises his voice: 'In a word, don't you realise that today God's salvation has come into Zacchaeus' life?'

Zacchaeus is a new man: saved by God's welcoming embrace, he is finally reconciled with himself and others. His humble wish to see Jesus has transformed his life: the smallest of seeds has become a large tree.

IN FAVOUR OF LIFE, BUT HOW?

That afternoon, on the banks of the Lake of Genessaret, a large crowd had gathered to listen to Jesus. They had come in great numbers from the nearby towns and villages, as happened only on big occasions. By now the sun was setting and a light breeze freshened the air. But no one noticed. They had much else to hold their attention. They were not even aware that time was getting on.

Jesus was speaking about very wonderful things. They had never heard the like, so clear and comforting. Then Jesus was speaking to them with an authority which gave them strength and security. It was soon apparent to them that his words were borne of a very special experience.

He was saying: 'Look at the beautiful flowers which brighten the fields around us. They are clothed in splendour. Who knows what kings and queens would give to be seen decked out like this. But they do not succeed: they are not able to be dressed in such a way. God clothes the flowers with a gesture of love freely given. Think how much each of us will worry, if we are too concerned with things that tomorrow will be burned up by the sun and vanish into nothing.'

It is strange they had never thought about it. And yet it's really like that. But it is not finished. Straight away Jesus adds: 'Look at the birds who fly in the air. Not one dies from hunger, even if they have neither barns nor means of help. God thinks to give each one what it needs. If he thinks so much about such young sparrows try to imagine the love he bears for each one of us. We are important to God. Everyone knows it. Moreover, God considers important those who are numbered just like a sparrow that flies in the air.'

He was listened to with delight. Time was passing and no one minded. Every word that left Jesus' mouth was like a welcoming embrace.

Only Jesus noticed that time was passing. Love comes to notice these things. He stops. He looks around. He seeks to take stock of what is going on. Then he decides to address Philip, who was nearby. 'Philip, let us break off for a few moments. These people deserve a little rest. Make use of the pause by giving them something to eat. Who knows how hungry these poor people are. They have journeyed far to get here and now they have taken in four hours' worth of conversation.'

Philip was lost for a moment. 'Jesus, there's no problem about having a break. But there's another problem: the bread to feed all these people.' Another disciple comes up: 'Jesus, I counted them while you were speaking. There are almost ten thousand. It's a record. Think how many loaves would be needed to fill even a hole in the stomachs of all these people!'

'What can be done?', Jesus insists to Philip. He doesn't have to wait for an answer, which is given with impeccable logic: ' The best solution is this: let's get to the end quickly and then send each one back to his own house. We have neither bread nor money. We are in a deserted place. There's really nothing to be done. Send the people home before it gets dark and...' He does not say 'It will be arranged' but he understands at once.

This does not suit Jesus at all. Philip has deceived him. He has been with him for a long time... and look at the result.

'Philip, your solution is absurd. I have spoken about the

Father who sustains the birds and clothes the lilies of the field and you advise me to finish speaking to these people and to send them home with empty bellies.' When speaking about God, Jesus first of all states the facts. He assures them that God is a good and welcoming Father, because he restores freedom to the poor sinner, life to the boy who died so young, and health to the woman doubled over by sickness.

Philip was confused. He did not really know which way to turn. His fellow disciples were also waiting, anxious and uncertain.

Jesus takes the initiative. He says to Philip: 'Check whether anyone has brought a loaf with them.' 'Has anyone brought some food with them?' shouts Philip.

A little boy comes forward carrying a little basket. 'I have five loaves and some fish. My mother gave them to me before leaving home. I was going to eat them, when I heard Philip calling. So here I am. What's up?'

Jesus stares at him with an enchanting look.

'Listen', he says, 'I want to make a bet with you. You give me all your provisions. We share them with this crowd. This is the wager: by sharing your bread, we satisfy everyone's hunger: you, me, Philip, my friends and all these people. Are you on?'

The boy is not sure. He is thinking about his loaves, his own hunger, the long journey to get home. He looks at the crowd: so many people. How can his five loaves be sufficient?

He returns the glance: he is generous, but not overly so. 'Jesus, let's divide it in two: some loaves for you and the rest for me. It's not an offer to turn down. Is that all right?'

Jesus is not happy with this. His request is very demanding: 'Everything'. Only in this way can everyone's hunger be satisfied 'If you don't want to, no problem. You take your loaves and eat them. It will not be easy. You will have hundreds of eyes watching you. Someone will try to take it away from you. You will have to defend yourself with your teeth. But the loaves are yours and you have the right to do what you want.'

Jesus insists: 'This is the bet: if you give them to me and we share them among everyone, there will be new life for all.'

The boy agrees. He gives Jesus his few loaves and the four fish. They begin to share them and to eat. The more they divide them up the more the bread and fishes increase. There is plenty for everyone: not just a mouthful but enough to fill the stomach.

Finally, they collect the scraps. The people's hunger has been satisfied and there are still seven full baskets left over.

Jesus finishes by saying: 'It is true: the Father feeds the birds of the air and clothes the lilies of the field. He alone does this. But to satisfy human hunger (the hunger for bread and the hunger for hope), he needs help. Life can grow in us only if one renounces one's possessions, sharing them, and giving them out of love. We have tried doing this tonight. Go home and do the same. Goodbye.'

The crowd disperses, thoughtful and perplexed.

They were used to hearing it said: 'Give up what you own. Make sacrifices. Think of those who suffer and learn to look for a little suffering yourselves, at least out of solidarity.'

Jesus turns the injunction on its head: 'I have come that all may have life and happiness. The Father wants us to have so much that we no longer know where to put it. God is like that: he feeds the birds of the air and clothes the flowers of the field, without seeking anything in return. He is happy to do it, and that's enough. He does it because he loves his children to the point of madness.'

But there is a 'but', hard and demanding.

Life increases only if someone knows how to give it out of love. If we hold on to it, we lose it ourselves and make others lose it. If we know how to share everything, yes everything, we will have life and happiness to the full.

Was Jesus right? Everything becomes more compelling.

It is not enough to give up something, nor is it sufficient to give to the poor what is left over and what we have not had the courage to throw away. Share everything in order to possess everything. Instead of dividing between what is mine and what is given to others, everything becomes mine if I share it with others. This is what Jesus offers in order to enjoy life and happiness.

Someone invented 'mortification' as an irrenounceable condition of education. It's an ugly expression and its essence is worse. To mortify means 'to give death.' Jesus wants life and happiness. He fights against death rather than seeking it and adopting it. But he lays down a very demanding condition: unless the grain of wheat should die, it neither lives nor gives life.

Wouldn't it be better to remove the expression 'mortification' from the dictionary of pastoral work and seek to replace it by the word (and action) 'sharing'?

4
The Way

Those who have the task of undertaking pastoral projects know that some forms of action are almost obligatory. Provision must always be made for them, even if the times and moments at which they take place can be varied. In the preceding pages I have mentioned some. We know very many others, without any need to call them to mind: by now they form part of that atmosphere within the Church which we experience with joy each day.

What Jesus puts before us is even more demanding. Not only does he ask us to lose nothing along the way, but he also urges us to do everything that is asked of us 'in a certain way.' In this case the quality is as important as the content.

It is not easy to give a firm outline of the characteristics of this way of doing things. Nevertheless, we cannot refuse since we are committed to making a list of the actions.

To help those who wish to engage in pastoral work seriously, I have re-read the Gospel in this disquieting yet encouraging way, in order to meet the necessary suggestions.

I put them forward again, as I have understood them, by telling some stories.

The Council of Jerusalem

In apostolic times the Church also found itself facing difficult problems. It discovered one possibility of responding through the 'intervention' of a Council. The Council of Jerusalem, the first in a long series, above all suggested criteria for confronting such questions.

Signs of faith

We must identify with Thomas. He was absent when the Risen Jesus appeared to the other disciples. He wants to see clearly in order to believe and then he teaches us to believe without demanding particular signs.

Wanting to separate good from evil

It was in the disciples' blood to want to separate good from evil. They had inherited it. But fortunately Jesus took a stand – for them and for us – calling us to adopt a very different approach when carrying out pastoral projects.

Read within

John's disciples were charged with reporting on who Jesus is and to what extent one could trust him. Jesus' response illustrates a fundamental demand of Christian experience: interpreting reality at different levels in order to arrive at the truth from the mystery within every event.

Real problems

Every pastoral project begins with a list of problems. But it is easy to invent problems in order to sell our own solutions. Jesus asks for the courage to distinguish real problems from false ones.

Who is the strongest?

Sometimes we discover that we are obliged to defend God's rights and we do so on the pretext of finding out that God is God because he is stronger than his enemies. And what if instead the stronger were the one who knows how to forgive?

THE COUNCIL OF JERUSALEM

Jesus had a very special way of communicating to his friends the things that were deepest in his heart: he continually intertwined actions and words.

Actions and words were never chosen at random, as with those people who do not want to compromise themselves and, moreover, sermonise on everything as if they owned the world.

What Jesus had at heart was life for all in God's name. He had come for this: he felt himself to be invested with a responsibility for taking people's breath away: reassuring everyone about God's love and his passion for life. The actions performed each day and the many words he spoke, these echoed like the long, happy refrain of this love song.

The disciples had put a lot into understanding him. They had been brought up on another image of God and with very different concerns. But by now, after the resurrection of Jesus, they had entered fully into this new and fascinating way of thinking. To complete their training and strengthen their vocation, Jesus, before leaving them, had given them his Spirit. Thus they too, like their master, now felt it their duty to proclaim, to their very last breath, the experience of God's love to everyone, by word and deed.

On occasions they appeared anew each day.

One thing, however, had left them rather perplexed.

It was a big problem: how to take on the law of Moses and the long series of religious traditions of the Jewish people?

Two very different categories of people were anxiously awaiting a reply.

Many good Jews had decided to remain with Jesus, because they recognised him as the Messiah of God, of whom their parents had spoken so much. Coming from the Jewish world and culture, they were used to observing all the mosaic laws. They did not feel overburdened, even if the laws were excessively detailed. They understood them from the inside and by now were sufficiently at their ease. But there was another question: all this, was it really necessary? To be disciples of Jesus, was it enough to continue being good observant Jews or else could Jesus' command to put the new wine into new wineskins hold true for this experience as well?

On the other hand, there were Christians who did not come from the Jewish world. Born and bred far from Jerusalem and Palestine, they had very different customs. They did not consider themselves bound to a chain of rather strange traditions. They used to eat everything. They did not carry out circumcision. They lived upright lives even without the obsession for ritual cleansing, the Sabbath and thousands of other purely Jewish usages. Once, they had even had a few laughs about it. And now? To be disciples of Jesus did they have to fit into this world? They were certainly well disposed to everyone: Jesus had by now filled their whole lives. In order not to lose him, they could relinquish some of their freedom. But was it necessary?

In replying to this question, the Church in Jerusalem found itself divided. Everyone was aware of the seriousness of the matter in terms of current practice. Today we might smile a little and have a ready answer to solve the problem. But they knew that there was a complicated balance between past and future and they recognised that the possible solutions would have to be tested if indeed it is in Jesus alone that we can have life and hope or if on the other hand there are other saviours as well as Jesus, as if he alone was not sufficient.

The disciples had discussed it at length. They were ready with the theoretical answer: only Jesus. Yet from Jesus' own teaching they had discovered that words were not enough, not even ones that were precise, sure and perfect. They wanted actions. Here they were more than a little shaky. It was a question of falling in with the world in which they had grown up, in which they had met Jesus, and in which they had shared promises and hopes.

Every now and then one of their inner circle, who had direct contact with the new disciples, strongly urged them: 'Have courage, decide. Things cannot go on like this, with feet in two camps. In this way arguments will arise, and they will be difficult to settle.'

Paul was one of them. A friend whom he had helped was not from the Jewish world and did not know the requirements and customs of the law of Moses. What was he to do? Was he to ask him to make the sacrifice of entering through this narrow door or should he leave him in peace, joyfully welcoming his missionary zeal?

At a certain point one of the hypotheses prevails: we discuss things together, openly. Peter summons a type of general assembly. All those who have a recognised responsibility in the Church take part: the original disciples and those who had been counted among their number subsequently. They didn't know it, but they had discovered one of the most important features in the life of the Church. Some centuries later someone would given a formal name to this event: the Council.

And so it was that the solution to this thorny problem was entrusted to the earliest Council in the history of the Church, the Council of Jerusalem. This first Council teaches many things.

The question is straightforward: only Jesus or Moses as well? Was there to be imposition of the law which every good Jew scrupulously observed down to the last letter, or was the Gospel sufficient?

But they do not begin to discuss it in theoretical terms, trying to split hairs. Jesus had never done this. He used to tell stories taken from daily life in order to speak about the most important and wonderful things. He spoke about sheep, good shepherds and mercenaries to whom it did not matter if the sheep met with an accident. He called to mind wedding feasts and hosts of excellent and somewhat presumptuous guests. He talked about lost and found coins, riches to be utilised and fields to be cultivated. Then, when words were no longer enough, he turned to actions: the lame walk, lepers are healed, the blind see, even the dead are raised and the poor hear good news for the first time.

The disciples at the Council also decide to follow the same method. The experience of having been with Jesus becomes the benchmark by which the problem is addressed and they look for solutions together.

Peter begins. He relates an experience which had shocked him. A few months ago at Jaffa he had been confronted with a disturbing choice. A newly-converted pagan had invited him to his house. Should he accept the invitation to sit at table with the man and his friends? He had never done so before and it seemed to him a betrayal of all his former observance of Jewish laws. Jesus' words resounded clearly but perhaps it was better to wait. A little caution would not go amiss. Suddenly he saw in front of him a table laden with food. There was everything on that table. A good Jew would run off in horror. 'Peter, come and eat, don't worry', says a mysterious voice as if from the table. He knows that it comes from above. He replies quite firmly: 'No, Lord. I have never done that. I'm certainly not going to do it now.' Peter was now very sure, just like old times. The voice insists: 'Eat. There is no such thing as good and bad foods. God has created and blessed everything. It is all his gift. We are brothers and sisters in God's love and because of the death and resurrection of Jesus.' Peter has overcome all resistance. He accepts the invitation. He enters the house of the newly-converted pagan and eats with him.

He relates this experience with great zeal. Everyone is convinced. Actions become eloquent words.

It is James who replies. He is a wise man, with the authority of his grey hair and his faith. He suggests a definite criterion. 'Jesus has made us discover by experience that God means well. We found this out because we tried. Peter had betrayed the master. Jesus taken him by the scruff of the neck in the name of God. And we are happy to have him among us, as an authoritative witness to the master.' He insists: 'We have tried so many times. This is what we must do: we solve our theological problems not by looking for the most correct answer, because it would be too difficult and we will never find a way out. Let us look for the solution which allows everyone to gain first hand experience that God means well and welcomes us with his embrace of peace.

He has got everyone to agree. No one has won: neither those who wanted a more liberal stance nor those who were resisting with all their might. The experience of love has triumphed. The proposed solution echoes like good news which gives direct experience of God's love.

The final document of the Council of Jerusalem says this with a solemn expression: 'We have decided, the Holy Spirit and ourselves, not to impose any further obligations other than those which are necessary: you are to abstain from flesh meat offered to idols, from blood, from the meat of strangled animals, and from immodesty. For that reason you will do well to guard against these things. Stay well' (Acts 15:28-29).

But it does not end here. Paul was there. He too rejoices at the decision reached by the Council. But he knows he will have to meet people bound by a strict observance of the law. They also have the right to experience God's welcoming love. They are going to be respected.

To the inhabitants of Galatia, divided between observants and revolutionaries, Paul speaks loud and clear: 'We are free. The cross of Christ has freed us from all laws. We have the duty and the right to live in freedom. Whoever does not know this or is afraid, compromises the power of the cross of Jesus.' However, in a letter addressed to the people of Corinth, Paul, using the logic of love, comes to an interpretation of the final Jerusalem document: 'I know that I can eat whatever I wish. My freedom has a precise limit beyond which I cannot go: it ends where the demands of love begin. For this reason, I assure my brothers that they would suffer if they saw me eating some prohibited food: I will not eat it forever. I cannot say that God loves us and welcomes us, when offending the sensibilities of some of my brethren' (1 Cor 8:9-13).

The Church went ahead with this criterion for such a long time. Then, with the strange logic of one step at a time, compromise and fear crept in. Fortunately, the most recent Council returned to the same spirit as that first one held in Jerusalem.

SIGNS OF FAITH

Jesus' violent death had unsettled his disciples. Some had packed their bags and set off home: they saw that the adventure had ended in the worst possible way. The only thing to do was to resume their normal pattern of life, in addition to a touch of nostalgia.

Another even lacked the courage for this kind of action, afraid of ending up by being laughed at, he who had looked everyone up and down haughtily on the day he had left to follow Jesus.

Quite a few had remained in Jerusalem, frightened to death. They had not gone out for days, hoping that as time passed things would calm down. Then, all of a sudden, something changed.

First some rumours, which were met with a good deal of scepticism. Then news that flashed like the lightening in a summer storm.

Now and again someone knocked hard on the door of the disciples' retreat: 'We have seen the Lord. He is alive, just as he promised. You remember that day when we saw him as if he had gone off his head. He was saying: you are giving me up to be killed, but do not think you have triumphed. I hand myself over to death, of my own free will; and it is still not finished: the Father will raise me to life. We did not really believe him then. We were saddened to hear him speak only of death. Now the facts are in his favour. He has appeared in glory. He is truly risen.'

'Are you sure?' 'I have seen him with my own eyes. He spoke to me.'

Faith was returning. They were beginning to ask themselves: 'Now then, what shall we do?'

On that night as well the question was pressing in on them: 'What shall we do?' Suddenly, without knocking and without opening the door, Jesus is standing among them. They were all there: 'It is I. I am with you, alive. I have conquered death forever. Think back to what we shared together. Now it is time to fulfil what we planned. Go, leave Jerusalem: make for the four corners of the earth.'

They were all there, all but one: Thomas was missing. He returns a few hours later. With great excitement they tell him what had happened. They all talk at once. They don't pay any heed to Thomas' pleas: 'Calm down, one at a time. What has happened? What did he say? Are you sure that it was really Jesus?'

They do not convince him. Thomas comes to a firm conclusion: 'I want to see him myself. On the contrary: I don't even trust the eyes. I want to touch. If it really is him, I wish to see his wounds.'

The discussion finished in this way. No one had persisted. 'And if Thomas was right?' There were still some doubts: 'We cannot risk another time. Jesus demands a great deal: go into all the world to proclaim the kingdom of God. Who will listen to us? They will demand some proof. And us, how are we to give it?'

Suddenly one evening, just like the first time, Jesus appears again among his disciples. This time Thomas is there as well. All of them are there.

Jesus goes straight up to Thomas: 'Greetings, Thomas. You were not completely wrong to look for proof. Here, look, see the marks of my wounds. It is really me: the one condemned to death risen by the power of God. Have courage, put your hand in my side. Are you convinced now?'

Thomas bursts into tears. He realises he has got everything wrong. Jesus has not rebuked him. He has even said he was right. This is the wonderful thing about Jesus: he gives you credit; he embraces you as if you were the best of all and then you are turned inside out, with an overwhelming desire to change your life.

Thomas reflected on so many instances where he had been a spectator. Sometimes they had not really sunk in. If it had depended on him... He remembers that time when Jesus had invited himself to a meal with a hardened sinner like Zacchaeus. And Zacchaeus sees all the errors of his ways and changes his life in a radical manner. The same had happened with the sinful woman, dragged by her feet to be stoned to death. Jesus treats her well: he throws her accusers into confusion and raises her to her feet, to look her straight in the eye. And that woman discovered the emptiness of her life and was changed. Now he too puts himself in the place of those who had judged. Like them, he bursts with the desire to change his way of thinking and living.

Thomas does not attempt to make any gesture. He no longer has any need to. He cries out so impulsively that everyone is taken aback: 'My Lord and my God. Thank you, Jesus. I bless you and adore you. I believe in you with all my life. I entrust myself to you.'

Jesus smiles at him: 'Well done, Thomas: this means that you believe. See: it is necessary to believe in the risk of the one who entrusts himself to a great mystery and surrenders himself in a vortex of love. You were looking for signs. I have given them to you. But it is doubtful whether it has been these that convinced you. Faith is something different: the result of signs is not certain.

'It applies to everyone', Jesus insists. 'This is the faith that I ask of my disciples: to trust God so much that they give themselves to him completely, like a child in its mother's arms. Certainly, God is a great mystery: this is why faith in him is always a little risky.

Do you want me to make a comparison? Think of a person who finds himself at the edge of a precipice and who wants to throw himself off. He knows that a friend is waiting for him, ready to catch hold of him. He has tried it so many times already but each time is like it was before. And what if something did not go well and in the place of the welcoming arms there were some rocky crags?'

The disciples are speechless. Jesus had hit the target. They were used to a different way of thinking. For them, as for every good Jew, to trust in God meant to surrender oneself to a powerful hand, ready to rout enemies.

Their thoughts turned spontaneously to Moses. God charges him to speak in his name and, to give him courage, he gives a series of powerful signs: the staff, which changes into a serpent and devours the serpents of the other sorcerers, the water which springs from the rock, the sea divided in two to allow his people to pass through.

They were thinking of Elijah who defies the priests of Baal. He ridicules them, wins over them and destroys them with the same fire that had consumed the sacrifice.

And now. Jesus proposes a very different way of doing things.

They recall the insults of those standing at the foot of the cross: 'If you are the Son of God, come down from the cross and we will believe in you.' They were expecting a wonderful gesture which would leave everyone gaping. And instead Jesus remained on the cross, vanquished by the wickedness of those whom he had loved and served.

The crisis had really begun at that time: 'Is it possible? It was the best, perhaps the last, occasion to understand who was right. It was not us.'

Instead Jesus draws outside the history of believing without looking for signs. It is not might that is right, but defeat. He allows himself to be put to death on the cross to show that he is truly the Son of God. So where are we?

Jesus' invitation to them has its own kind of folly. They talk about it often. They want to understand a little better. One day Mary the mother of Jesus was also among them: 'What do you say about it, Mary? Must we really learn to believe without seeking any signs?'

Mary did not hesitate, even for a split second. 'Certainly: this is the only way of living by faith. I too have been through it. I too have struggled hard to convince myself. But there really isn't any other way. Jesus has gone that way continually.'

And she recalled: 'Before you were around I was living in Nazareth, quietly and without any great plans. An angel of God asked me if I was willing to become the mother of Jesus. I was taken aback. Me, the mother of God? I who, among other things, had decided to remain a virgin. The angel had said to me: Trust in God. I understood nothing. But I replied: Of course I trust. I am the servant of the Lord. This is how Jesus was born.'

The disciples are astonished. Mary continues: 'Shortly after the birth of Jesus, I took him to the temple for the purification. Do you know what happened to me? An old man took Jesus in his arms and said very strange things about him. They were about me and him: Jesus is a sign of contradiction: a sword will pierce my soul. I understood it much later, a little at a time. Only at the foot of the cross did it become completely clear. But that day I offered God my trust in him. I did it blindly, leaping into the very depths of the mystery.

WANTING TO SEPARATE GOOD
FROM EVIL

Jesus was walking with his disciples and at the same time was chatting with them about the things closest to his heart. He often used to do this. He did not like sitting in a chair and asking his listeners to sit down quietly at his feet like so many schoolchildren. He had not obtained his authority by a system of appointments or through outward insignia. This is what the doctors of the law had done. But they did not like him very much: he gave the impression that he was above things. The authority to say the things he said came to him out of the courageous sincerity with which he spoke, from a boundless zeal for the life of all and, above all else, from that somewhat mysterious knowledge that was called 'the experience of the Father', leaving the sceptics in dismay.

That day he had chosen to take a stroll in the countryside, among the hills which went down towards the lake. By now the wheat in the fields was growing firm and strong. But here and there the ground was stained a strange colour. Among the ears of corn patches of weed were appearing, an odious type of grass which ruined everything. To have gathered it with the wheat and ground it in the mill would have made the bread inedible, and it would have to be thrown out ruthlessly.

Here and there some tufts had sprouted on their own after each sowing. But this time it didn't take much to see that it had been done by the hand of enemy. How awful: they had been sown on purpose, a few days after the proper sowing, to insult those who had left their mark. He had disappeared without trace. Only now, some months after the deed was done, was the disaster taking hold.

Jesus was speaking. But the disciples were paying little attention to him. They were distracted. They were disturbed at seeing those cornfields full of weeds. They had to do something. It was a bit risky to take some action now but it was better to take that risk now before it was too late.

Eventually one of the disciples spoke on behalf of everyone. 'Jesus', he says, interrupting him sharply, 'you have seen what a disaster this is. Perhaps the owner is still not aware of it. Things are going badly. Too many weeds are growing with the good wheat. The harvest will be a disaster.' 'I too am aware of it. I am not blind. An evil man has wanted to take revenge. This is what happens in life: if we are not careful and don't remain vigilant, the devil comes and destroys what we have built.'

Jesus has put it in the context of life and its demands.

The disciples are not content with this. The disaster is too serious. There is a need to do something. 'Listen Jesus, we agree about the devil and being vigilant but things here have taken a turn for the worse. Let us stop and lend a hand to the poor landowner.'

They had a good and detailed plan. 'We give him a hand. We help him, just as you have taught us so many times.' They insist: 'With all the care we can muster, let's go into the field, root out the weeds and clear them away. Now there is still time: in a few weeks it will be too late.'

They expect Jesus to praise them.

Their mouths drop when, in a low voice, Jesus replies: 'Do nothing. Are you mad? Which of you knows wheat from weeds? You are fishermen. With your faulty knowledge and in all your enthusiasm, you will pluck the good wheat and the weeds at the same time. You would end up making things far worse that the evil you are trying to put right. Let's continue along our road. Let the wheat and the weeds grow together and see what will happen

The disciples are not happy with this. They feel useless and must give up their truly generous willingness to lend a hand. Under their breath they are muttering: 'But it does not end here: now we are showing ourselves up in front of Jesus.'

They continue on their way. They head for the shore of the lake. The fields have already taken them in that direction. They had only to quicken their steps and they had arrived there at once. They were in the trade: they knew that this was more or less the time at which the fishermen would have returned to the shore, their nets full of fish. They had done it themselves so many times: the boats down to the waterline. A quick check on the size of the catch and then the good fish put into baskets and sent quickly to the market and the poor ones thrown back into the water as bait for the next catch.

A knowing look quickly given, more eloquent than thousands of words: even the fish must be separated into good and bad, just as they had wanted to do with the stalks of corn earlier on. But these are fish. This needs the expertise and eye of the fisherman, and we – the look says it all – are among the best on the lake, even if we have left our boats and nets to follow Jesus.

They were thinking: 'We can lend a hand to our friends. They will be very happy with that, since it will lighten their load. This time we want to see if Jesus tells us that this is not our business.'

They are at the shore in an instant. There are three boats, unbelievably full of fish. The disciples go near, while Jesus continues to be indifferent.

'Nice fish, aren't they?' 'We cannot really complain. There's still a bit of work, the usual, and then we go to the market with it and straight home to rest for a while.' 'If you like, we'll give you some help to sort the good fish to be sold from the bad ones to be thrown back into the sea. Jesus, what do you say? Shall we lend them a hand? We'll save a bit of time.' Perhaps someone will also have thought to himself: 'We are doing a good job like this as you are always telling us to do.'

All eyes fell on Jesus. Someone whispered: 'And don't make the excuse that we're not experts: we are on home territory here.'

No one had expected Jesus to reply in the way he did. It stung like vinegar sprayed onto a wound. 'That's enough, please, of this rash desire to separate into good and evil. That at first was an excuse. It is not a question of expertise. It is a different matter, much more demanding. I want my disciples to be free from the temptation to judge and to divide. If one spends one's time separating good from bad, how are one's actions going to proclaim that God first loves everyone without staring them in the face and without asking anything beforehand?

When he sends the rain or the heat of the sun, he does not distinguish between the good man's field or the house of the wicked. He sends the same gift to all, with the same intensity. God is a loving Father who cares for his children: all are his children.'

On that occasion Jesus finished like this, cutting short his disciples' instinctive desire to separate into good and bad. The discussion seemed to have drawn to a close. But it was not completely closed. One day Jesus himself returned to the subject, taking it to quite impossible lengths in the opinion of his disciples, who as good Jews were used to a different style of debate. He had said, with the same authority with which he had told them not to separate into good and bad: 'Look, if you really refrain from making classifications and you wish to pay special attention to some types of people, well, in that case, give all the preference you wish to those who don't usually matter very much. The Samaritans – everyone, not excluding anyone, not only the very fine person in the story that I told you one day sinners and outcasts, even prostitutes have a special place in God's love.' 'Is that possible?', the disciples exclaimed with open eyes, astonished and a little scandalised. 'In that case it is better to be this sort of bad person, rather than keep the law and respect the traditions.'

Jesus reinforces what he has said: 'You must not get into the habit of judging who is better and who is worse. Words may change, but attitudes remain the same. The real question is this: who is more loved according to the plan of God's gratuitous love? It concerns God and not the quality of people's lives. This is the beauty of things. It could not work like this if at the root of everything we had any claim to merit, but there is only a love as vast as the star-studded heavens.'

Someone is still a little suspicious. He thinks: 'It would be very nice if it were true. Can it be true?'

Jesus is aware of this. He replies in his own way: 'The Father has sent me to pasture his flock. He has all the sheep very much at heart: all of them, bar none. I cannot behave like the mercenary, who is motivated by a concern for payment and not the interests of the sheep. He runs away when faced with danger: first the hide and then the rest. But not me. I give my life for my sheep.

If one sheep runs off in search of adventure, I do not condemn it but I run after it, with the great effort that comes from love. Think about it: the good shepherd, who loves his own sheep, is ready to leave the ninety-nine good ones in the sheepfold to run breathlessly in search of the one that is lost.

This means classifying things according to the laws of love: pride of place goes to the one in need, the one in danger, the one who is far off. Finally, a great feast is held for the sinner who allows himself to be enfolded in love: a much greater feast than that reserved for the just who are always close by and do not have fanciful ideas in their head.'

The disciples have at last understood Jesus' command not to divide into good and bad. The issue is not to do with the spoiled wheat nor the unsuitable fish. It was about the children of God. Jesus does not want distinctions that turn into dangerous forms of discrimination. He bids us go out to those who are most in need. If we really want to separate or divide, so as not to make any distinctions, the benefit of the doubt goes immediately to the one who is in greater need of a welcoming embrace. The disciples had finally understood. What about us?

READ WITHIN

John had ended up in prison. He had foreseen it: to say in forceful terms to one so powerful what he deserved was always going to lead to this outcome.

Then he had been hard, presumptuous and shameless with Herod. He had told him straight to his face: 'It is not enough to give orders on the presumption that you are able to do what you like. You cannot take your brother's wife.

Send her home and change your way of living. If you do not, you are finished.'

Herod was afraid of John. He considered him to be one of lowest of the low, who did not submit to his every whim. But he was unable to allow him to get away with such a blatant offence. He had his dignity to uphold. And so he had John thrown into a maximum security prison. He had made John understand that there was only one way out: to ask for pardon publicly and to join the mainstream, respecting (as he himself thought) his dignity and his responsibilities. Basically, he was thinking to mind his own business and not to interfere in that of others. That never does any harm.

In his prison cell John was reflecting on the meaning of his own life. He knew he was sentenced to death. Perhaps Herod would not reach a decision straight away. But Herodias, that good-for-nothing who had seduced Herod, was fanning the flames, convinced that the only solution was to get rid of John, and the sooner the better.

He did not even address the question of asking pardon of Herod, committing himself to having to sing his virtues out of love for the kingdom. John knew him very well: he could save his skin and even secure a place of honour at court, but he would bring about an inner death, the sad accompaniment to a serious betrayal.

He knew he was condemned to death.

One day his disciples go to visit him in prison. They speak to him about Jesus. 'John, do you know that there's someone going around who says he knows you and often speaks well of you. We have heard him many times. He speaks about wonderful things in a more pleasant and forceful tone even than yours. The people listen to him and follow him. Ah, you know, one day this man said: "If anyone trusts in me, he will not die. I have conquered death. Whoever listens to my words has life." Think about it, John, if it were true...'

John knew Jesus. He was even related to him. Above all

he knew he had a specific task to fulfil concerning Jesus. But all this about life in his name looked to him to be rather new. And was it true? 'In your view', John asks, 'can it be true? Can I die in his name and be sure of having life?' His disciples are not certain: 'We do not know. If you want, we will go and look for him, speak to him about your problems and your doubts. We will ask him for confirmation. Do you want that?'

They leave straight away, after bidding a quick farewell, bearing John's reply.

They look for Jesus. They find him and speak to him face to face.

'Jesus, John is languishing in Herod's prison. He needs a word of encouragement. You are the life: you say that whoever has faith in you has life. Is it true or are they only words? What life do you offer to your friend John?' They press the point: 'Tell us who you are and we will run back to consult John. He is waiting anxiously, staring death in the face.'

Jesus replies straight away. This is a chance not to be missed. John deserves this and much more.

'Do you want to know who I am and if you can trust my words? I haven't just spoken words. My words are deeds. Look around you: the blind see, the lame walk, the lepers have skin as smooth as a child's, the dead are raised up, the poor, for whom no one cares, are those who first receive the good news.' Jesus speaks about himself by giving a long list of his works. Now and then, someone in the crowd raises his voice: 'It is true! There was no life in my legs and my hope too was dead. I had been at the side of the pool for years. No one was helping me to go in when the angel stirred the water. And Jesus came by. He solved the problem with one glance. Look, I am well! As well as the water in the pool, he has healed me.' Others echoed this: 'I too was blind: someone told me that Jesus was passing by. I called out to him with all my voice. Now I can see perfectly well. I have life to the full.'

John's disciples were dumbfounded. They thought carefully about going back to their master. They were ready with an answer: 'John, you can put your faith in Jesus. Before saying what he says, he does it. Wherever he is, life really triumphs over death.'

Jesus blocked their path. 'Stop: wait a minute. I have not finished telling you what you must report back to John. It applies to everyone, not only him. Listen carefully.' They stop, amazed and a little curious. Jesus adds these words, speaking loudly so that everyone can hear.

'Tell John all the facts. But do not forget to add this: blessed are those who know how to interpret these facts and discover the reasons for hope behind them.' John's disciples are disturbed by this. They are petrified. 'What does this mean? What are we to say to the master?' Jesus reassures them: 'Do not worry: just tell him. John will understand. Give him my greetings and encourage him. John is a brave man, a great figure. No one is greater than him. He will understand, don't worry.'

Jesus was right. John understood only too well. And he died, killed by the violent action of the tyrant, for Jesus' sake. Now he is alive. We remember him like one who is living.

What did Jesus want?

The invitation to read within or inside recurs so very often in the experience of Jesus.

One day he was walking through a valley with his disciples. At a certain point he suddenly stops. He says: 'We must change our route. Let's go up to that isolated hamlet at the top of the hill. It is called Nain, do you know it?' 'Why, Jesus, this sudden change of plan?' Jesus has his reasons. At Nain the only son of a widow had been snatched away by death. They were taking him for burial. Everyone was in tears. Jesus can't bear to see it. He does not succeed in giving a reason for the death, he who seeks life for all. He changes direction. He hurries to Nain, dragging the bewildered disciples after him. The funeral cortege stops.

Jesus calls the boy by his name and returns him alive into his mother's arms.

The woman wipes away the last of her tears and looks at him with great warmth: 'Jesus, thank you. How blessed it is that your mother had a son like you. Give her my name. More than that: I want to get to know her and thank her in person.'

Jesus accepts her thanks. There is an exchange of greetings and wishes. But then he adds immediately, in the forthright manner that they all know so well: 'Together let us thank the Father in heaven. He feeds the birds of the air and clothes the lilies of the field. He wants life. I have come that all may have life.'

He seems to be saying this: the son who is returned to his mother's arms is only a sign, a sign as great as God's love, a sign of who God is for us. It is not enough simply to note the miraculous deed. It is necessary to read within, to interpret it, to grasp the mystery hidden among its folds. 'I have spoken to you about God', Jesus adds: 'I have done it in the way I like. I have offered you a sign of life, to make it easier for you to discover who God is for us.' And he concludes by saying: 'Rejoice in your son who has been restored to life and contemplate the mystery of God in his smiling face. Together we have reconstructed the mysterious face of God, restoring the smile to you and your son.'

This time it was easy. The widow of Nain and her fellow villagers had been fortunate: there is a direct and immediate relationship between God and life, the victor over death.

Less straightforward was their encounter with those poor people who were selling doves and goats in front of the temple and the others who had set up a money-changing stall in the nearby corner.

Jesus arrives, his eyes aflame. He takes some cord and makes a whip, and he goes down there, lashing out to left and right. He overturns everything like a madman.

Read within, interpret the inner meaning: an almost

desperate task. It is much more logical to stop at what he sees. Someone has said it: 'Finally we have found out whose side Jesus is on. He wants to be a revolutionary. Even with him the power to dominate is there. Let us join him and destroy everything. This is a good chance.' Jesus does not respond. He is just very sad. They haven't understood anything: they have stopped at the facts without any ability to read within, to interpret.

What is it with Jesus, overturning the stalls of the traders and moneychangers?

It was difficult to explain such an unforeseen action. Jesus has laid hold of people who were going about their own business. They were not breaking the law. The head of the temple had placed them there. The former, those who were selling turtledoves and other animals, were providing a service for those who went up to the temple to thank God for the birth of a new son. Mary had done the same with Jesus: a pair of turtledoves had had to be bought, because this was required of the poor, in order to thank God for the birth of Jesus. Even the money-changers were employed by the temple. They had charge of changing money for pilgrims, to enable them to make temple offerings in the one 'recognised' currency of God (according to Jewish tradition). They made their living one way or the other: and Jesus threw everything in the air. Why?

Today we are better able to read within. The full story of Jesus helps us.

Jesus came to tell everyone that God is the father of all. He loves first and asks nothing in exchange. He loves, and that's it. He loves everyone with a love that is freely given. Everyone: yes, everyone.

The law, which the money-changers and other traders served, taught the opposite: God gives life and one gets one's due; God has a watchful eye only for the Jewish people, he knows only their language and recognises their currency alone.

Jesus loses his temper. After having said again and

again what God is like, he attempts the way of actions. He almost seems to be saying: 'At last, have you decided on a good turn and discovered the true face of God?'

It is the same thing repeated: with John's disciples, with the grieving mother at Nain and with the money-changers at the temple in Jerusalem. There is only one problem: understanding is given only to those who are capable of reading within and risking an interpretation of the facts which has the full flavour of faith.

REAL PROBLEMS

There was a large crowd that day. Jesus had ended up right in the middle of it. The poor disciples were struggling like mad to let him have some breathing space. But they were not succeeding. Jesus was being pulled from every side. Everyone wanted to see him close up, touch him, speak to him face to face.

Suddenly Jesus is taken unawares. He seems to be concentrating on something else. Then he murmurs: 'Who touched me?' They look at him half seriously and half amused. Peter puts the question: 'Jesus, you want to know who touched you? Look around you. Everyone is touching you. And you want to know who touched you? Please, let's get out of this hell. Send them away, as quickly as possible, otherwise we'll all be driven mad.'

Jesus insists: 'Someone has touched me. I felt a shiver. I saw death take flight, conquered by life.'

From the background a woman's voice called out. The others fell silent and relaxed the pressure a little. 'Jesus, it was me. I did not touch you, because I didn't succeed in doing so. But I very much wanted to. I knew that if I could touch the hem of your cloak, I could be healed. I am sick. I have no more hope. You were my last hope. Now I know that I am healed. I feel it. Everything has changed. Jesus, you have healed me. Thank you, Jesus.'

She had wanted to touch Jesus in order to have that life which was escaping her. She had not managed to do it. But Jesus was aware of it and anticipated it. He accepts the hand she stretches towards him, without her needing to press. He anticipates her cry, though it is muffled, and he acts.

Life does not leave him indifferent. He has a passion for it. He cannot stand by and do nothing: that's the way he is. His friends too would have to be like him: the same zest for life and the same ability to notice straight away every raised hand looking for comfort.

But it is not easy to pick up the cry that life makes. It is often muffled and feeble; sometimes it is disturbed by strange signs that focus attention elsewhere.

Jesus' zeal for life, which he entrusts to his friends, really stems from the need to put things right, identifying problems both great and small, overcoming the temptation to allow what is small and trifling to become too large and closing one's eyes to what is more serious and alarming.

Time and again this is what Jesus himself teaches.

That day he had brought the disciples in front of the temple treasury at the very moment that people with bulging wallets were coming to place alms in the offertory box.

There was a long queue in front of the treasury box just then. Everyone was putting something in. They did so ostentatiously, gaining approval and causing astonishment. They put the money in, one after another, making very sure that the coins jangled as they fell into the bronze chest.

The disciples were rubbing their eyes but Jesus did not turn a hair. They thought it strange, because he always had something to say about everything and this time he says nothing. Damn it all, it would have been as well to make a few positive remarks. These are fine people, they keep the law and they are generous. They love the temple and support it by paying the proper taxes.

Jesus continued to talk about different things. He was wasting his breath. None of the disciples was listening to him any more, but concentrated instead on this wonderful sight of religious devotion.

Finally, the queue tailed off. The latecomers arrived, all concerned to regain people's attention with the sweet sound of their own offerings.

It is quiet again.

The disciples rejoin Jesus and take up the thread of the conversation.

Then, all of a sudden, he interrupts: 'I bet you haven't noticed anything.' 'What should we have noticed?', asked the good disciples in surprise.

They held their arms open towards Jesus. He had done everything to get the disciples used to changing the way they thought. He had not been very subtle about it. 'If you seek the places of honour, you will come to a bad end. They will take you by the collar and pursue you to the last, because sooner or later someone more important than you will come along. You will have to give up your place and everyone will mock you.' 'Do you want to be important? Who is the greater: the landowner who is sitting down at ease with his friends or the servant who concerns himself with his work?' The answer was very easy: there is no comparison between the servant and his master. Jesus replies very dryly, taking them aback: 'That's right, the landowner is the more important. Now tell me, why have I decided to be the servant of all? I put on the apron and begin to serve: not only at table, but in life. My service will end in the sacrifice of my life.'

Alas, everything has to be done all over again. Things have turned out to be very discouraging. The old way of thinking is putting up a struggle

Jesus' attention had been caught by something which no one else had noticed: there appeared an old woman who had been hidden from view. She too was giving alms to the temple. Sadly, she was very hard up. She had found only a few small coins. She had denied herself something to eat. She placed the coins in the treasury chest, feeling so ashamed, making very sure that she was not noticed. However, a bit of small change does not really make much noise. They only one who noticed her was the man responsible for emptying the chest at the end of the service. 'It has gone well: a day to remember. What's this? A few coppers? Some madman? Who is so hard up that they can spare only a few coins in almsgiving? It's just as well that there is still a religious spirit and that the books balance. If it were down to the generosity of these wretched people, we would have to shut up shop.'

Jesus' comments are of a completely different vein.

Only he had noticed the poor old woman. He brought her to the attention of his distracted disciples, who were captivated by the large amounts of money being deposited. Now at last he gives his judgement. 'Pay attention: that old woman has given more than everyone.' They correct him: 'We say the facts are different. When the money is counted, she will have put in less than the others. It's just that she did so with love and devotion. Let's pretend that it's more than the others.' Jesus will have none of it. This is not his way of thinking. If it was, to be greater than the others she would have had to impress them and have everyone pay their respects.

Jesus has a different way of reckoning: 'She has given more than everyone: the unit of currency is not to do with money. It is weighed in terms of love and willingness. This is the way of thinking in kingdom of heaven. Call it strange if you will, but that's how it is.'

Only by this way of looking at things can we place ourselves at the service of life: to discover where the problems really lie, and in order to decide the means by which the triumph of life is to be promoted.

'Unless the grain of wheat falls upon the ground and dies, it does not bear fruit. But if it dies, it bears much fruit. I assure you, whoever loves his own life will lose it. Whoever is ready to lose his life in this world will keep it unto eternal life' (Jn 12:24-25).

WHO IS THE STRONGEST?

It was a really difficult moment. The whole thing was an irreligious farce: they had condemned him to death, even before they had begun to judge him.

Jesus was alone, standing against everyone, guilty of having wanted the best for people and of having challenged those forms of behaviour, sadly so widespread, which imposed tyranny and injustice, and destroyed dignity, all in God's name.

He tried to defend himself. It was not his desire to demonstrate that he was right. He was trying, with the little energy he had left, to free his accusers from the web of death in which they had entangled themselves.

The chief priest wants to reach a quick conclusion. He tries to nail Jesus with his own words. If in front of everyone he declares he is the son of God in person that would be it. Everyone would be able to hear the blasphemy. Any lingering doubts would vanish and it would be the logical consequence that he be condemned to death. It would be right and fitting. The law requires it. There is no doubt about it, no problem at all. This is how they interrogate him about his ideas and plans.

Jesus does not fall into the trap. In a faint voice he replies: 'Why do you ask me these things? I have always spoken loud and clear. So many people have heard me. Ask them about it. They can tell you word for word what I said. Ask the lame whom I have healed. Question those poor lepers who have been thrown out of their own homes and who came back to their towns having been healed. Try to listen to the views of the poor and the outcasts, who find their hearts full of hope. Try to listen...'

He must be interrupted.

One of the crowd speaks out ferociously, as if he was trying to quash a show of rebellion. 'Is this how you answer the chief priest?' And he gave him a very hard blow. Jesus' face, which was already full of wounds, started to bleed again.

This servant of the chief priest was a terrible man: he hopes to make a career for himself regardless of the cost. He has found just the right occasion and throws himself headlong into it, like a vulture intent upon its prey.

Jesus looks at him pointedly. His eye can still see, even if his swollen face is flowing with blood.

Everyone stops. They wait.

One of them remembers one of Jesus' most memorable sayings: 'If someone strikes you on the right cheek, present the left cheek as well.' They were used to the logic of an eye for an eye. Everyone had taken note of Jesus' strange and disturbing command as never before.

'What is Jesus doing now: let's see if he presents the other cheek as he has said. This is the proof of the pudding. Let's see.'

It is not for nothing that Jesus offers his body to receive fresh insults and blows. His voice comes back sound and strong.

'Why have you beaten me? It is an unjust action. They have accused me and I defend myself. You have no right to strike me.' There is another pause. And then what?

Jesus repeats what he has said, with an authority which resembles those times when the crowds used to listen to him and hang upon his every word.

He turns to the cowardly servant. But he speaks to everyone. They all look away from him, that's for sure. 'You think you are stronger but you beat a man bound like a criminal. You are wrong. Here it is I who am the strongest.

Make sure you remember it, you and your friends. If I want to, I can cause a host of angels to come down from heaven. They are ready to set me free. Things would change immediately. Such happens to the kings of this world. I too am a king. I too have my army, ready to fight on my behalf. But this is not the way I think.

I am much stronger. Do you want me to prove it? So be it: I forgive you and all my accusers. I allow myself to be condemned unjustly. I have decided this. It is not you who will put me to death. I will it. This shows who is the strongest.'

Jesus has not closed his eyes to tyranny. He has never done so. He certainly cannot do it now, at the point of death, when every word and action weighs like a block of stone. Jesus forgives after having denounced evil and accused the wrongdoer. His forgiveness is neither rescinded not ineffective. It is a very powerful act of denunciation and accusation. It is a solemn gesture of freedom and love.

Much later they drag him up to Calvary and nail him to the cross. He is dying, suspended from a piece of wood between two criminals. They were thinking they had defeated and destroyed him. They had anxiously awaited this moment. They had finally brought him to submission, annihilated. They could carry on with their theological speculations. They could continue to rage at the poor people in God's name. No one would dare to stand up to them anymore.

A kind and good person played the last card. Is it possible that God does nothing for poor Jesus? He has not deserved this wretched death.

He cries out, risking his own reputation: 'We do not want to kill the innocent. If you are really the son of God, show it. There is still time. Come down from the cross, with a striking gesture. God would do this. We will believe you, all of us. You are safe and you have convinced us. Come down from the cross.'

He had a pretty good idea about God. God is much

stronger than his enemies. He destroys them. If Jesus is the son of God, he must demonstrate it by a show of strength.

This was what the man was really thinking. Everyone was thinking the same. They remembered Elijah, the prophet whose words were like thunder. In God's name he defied the priests of Baal. He had defeated them, put them to flight, enveloped in the all-consuming fire. They were thinking of Moses, the powerful hand of God: he made his way by governing and defeating. This is God... Jesus... let us see who is the stronger.

Jesus replies in his own way. He remains on the cross. He extends his arms in an embrace which encompasses everyone and all are immersed in life and hope.

He is the strongest, because the God of Jesus shows he is stronger than his enemies, by welcoming and forgiving. His embrace of peace is more powerful than the devouring fire, the whirlwind, the sword of justice.

Jesus had foretold it, seeking to explain his presence in the world. They had not understood. His way of thinking was too different from the norm, scandalous to the moderates, both Jews and Greeks.

One day a long time before, when things had seemed to be going the right way and the people clapped their hands and his disciples were beginning to make some plans for the future, Jesus had told a very strange story.

The owner of a vineyard sends his servants to the tenants to get from them what he was owed, according to the conventions of the day. But on that occasion things go badly. The servants returned empty-handed and badly bruised. The tenants rebelled. They handed nothing over and replied with violence.

The landowner is enraged. 'One must teach them a lesson to remember. Things cannot go on like this.' He seeks help and organises an armed expedition to punish the tenants. But the tenants were also organising themselves. They attempted to ambush the soldiers and destroyed the whole of that small army.

This is too much. The owner of the vineyard asks advice on planning the perfect form of punishment. He must show who is the strongest.

His counsellors come up with all the punishments in the book. He rejects them all; he doesn't consider them to be sufficient. They could leave some doubt as to who is the strongest.

He makes a decision by himself. 'I am sending my son.' 'You are mad! They will kill him straight away and everything will be finished. They will definitely become the strongest.'

To everyone's amazement the owner of the vineyard insists on it: 'I will show you. They are not the strongest if they kill my son as well. I am the strongest because I trust them, despite everything. The death of my son is the beginning of new life for everyone, even for his assassins.'

Then someone smiled. 'Poor thing, he is an illusion. That is the wrong with all the prophets. It's a shame... otherwise he is even agreeable.' Now someone remembers it. The story of the vine-dressers echoes like a whistling wind, while the sky is lit up by the flash of lightning and the veil of the temple is rent in two.

Jesus forgives and dies: he is the strongest. Once and for all, he has taught how life and hope triumph.

5
The Difficulties

We have all seen it so many times: the greatest enthusiasm sinks beneath the weight of difficulties. Some are external, unforeseen and disconcerting. Others, the worst sort, come from ourselves and block out everything, threatening the things in which we had placed so much hope. What is to be done?

A good project cannot ignore this scenario. On the contrary, it must take it into account as it is planned and carried out.

We must deal with difficulties as they arise, but of course we cannot anticipate the possible solutions with any great certainty. But we can foresee some paths of action, using them to challenge our own stories.

I have collected some stories from the Gospels: they suggest problems, uncertainties, and even betrayals of the kind which threaten every pastoral worker; but above all, they set out the directions with which all these can be solved.

How did it go?

It is often the case that good will which would move mountains is matched by poor results, and sometimes even by disaster. It is quite natural to ask the reason for all this and where the ultimate responsibility lies. A good pastoral project, which pays attention to the future, cannot but find itself facing problems of this kind. The Gospel suggests a 'strange' reply: the parable of the sower.

Do not be afraid

In the darkest moments – which are never lacking in the experiences of one who spreads the Gospel – we too cry out with the disciples on the boat, tossed by the stormy sea: Jesus, where are you? The reply: an almost unrecognisable ghost who draws near by walking on the billowing waves.

If your heart be troubled

If it was enough simply to declare one's own enthusiasm, we would have half the world already. But as experience proves, betrayal and fear are always nestling in the nooks and crannies of our existence. We are consoled by Peter's experience: even the worst form of betrayal becomes something that can be shared with others in order to build up hope.

A school of prayer

The story of the disciples on the way to Emmaus teaches us a lesson: it is only a short step from the generous 'yes' to discouragement. Jesus walks with us to restore our zeal and our hope.

HOW DID IT GO?

'How did it go?' is an obligatory form of greeting with which we welcome those who return from having carried out a task.

Whoever is asked a question of this kind has the chance of flattering himself a little, listing all the difficulties he has had to overcome and the accolades he has won. And it is put to others: to friends, as consolation for something unforeseen; those who are envious and jealous, to force them to admit that even for them things have gone really well on very many other occasions.

His disciples had never asked Jesus how he had got on. Everyone could see what he was doing. They would have received a rebuttal: 'Why are you asking me? Look around you and ask those who have listened to me. I speak openly, in the synagogues and in the temple. I don't have any secrets. What I have to say, I proclaim quite openly.'

But the question was often put to them with an ever greater insistence, as they returned from the missionary tours on which Jesus used to send his disciples.

'How did it go?' The reply was always this: 'Oh not bad, but of course not that good. Who knows why?' They put so much effort and care into it. They used up time, sleep and energy. Unfortunately, however, the results were not the most promising. Few of them were listening. Few asked themselves very deep questions and made a firm commitment to follow the young teacher from Nazareth. The miracles? Not even a faint shadow. The few times that they had attempted them, they had to flee, before the crowd came upon them with insults and blows. To tell the truth, one occasion went better than usual. But Jesus had thought to dampen their enthusiasm: 'I saw the devil rushing towards you. You had encouraged him by your presumption.'

In a meeting at which they reviewed matters and in which their faces were more tense than usual, a note of crisis was creeping into the air and they decide to face up to the problem. They are no longer able to accept half-measures and invitations to be patient. 'Jesus, help us understand. The mission you entrust to us is failing: zeal, diligence, hard work and no results. How is this possible?'

Jesus waits to answer. He is convinced that the silence helps to uncover prejudices, even those hidden in the deepest recesses.

The disciples come back at him again, disillusioned and gloomy: 'Please, Jesus, say something. Look: we cannot go on like this. Whose fault is it that we have failed? If we are not up to this task, never mind, we give it up once and for all. We are going back to our boats. At least there, it is easy to see the results of our labours.'

At long last the question is clear: who is to blame? Something hasn't gone according to plan: therefore there must be someone to blame in some way.

Jesus begins to speak. He looks towards the skies. The

poor disciples understand that this is half the reason for their vocation.

'Have you noticed what the farmer does when the season for sowing arrives? He gets ready, takes a sack of seed and goes out to the field. He puts a little of the seed in his apron and begins to scatter it to the four winds.

He has a long job. His actions are precise and sure. Unfortunately, it is difficult to account for the direction of the wind. Some seed falls on ground which has just been ploughed. It takes root and grows strong in the rich earth. But other seed falls on the edge of the field. The ground is too dry for the seed to flourish. A few handfuls of seed even fall among the stones which mark the boundary of the farm.

The birds are always hungry and are on the scrounge. They swoop down on the field in great flocks and fill their bellies with seed. Above all, the seed which falls at the edge of the field and that scattered on the stony ground soon becomes food for the birds.'

The story told by Jesus consoles them and worries them too. The sower is a fine sort, the seed is good, the ground is suitable. It is not his fault that some of the results are poor and uncertain. So who is responsible?

They know very well how the story ends.

Many months later the farmer reaps the rewards of his labours. He knows already that he cannot expect anything from the seed which fell beyond the area under cultivation. Even those few seeds which succeeded in taking root, resisting the assaults from the birds and the dryness of the soil, produced stunted ears of corn which are burnt up by the first sunshine of spring.

Yet Jesus insists: 'The story of the sower is only a parable. It makes us think about another type of sowing, one that is far more important: the word of God. What I am saying about the sower, applies above all to the one who goes forth to proclaim the kingdom of God. Think carefully about this.

The same ear of corn does not correspond to every grain sown. Sometimes an improbably large ear of corn grows from a grain; at other times, however, the ear of corn is slender and fearfully shrivelled. There are grains that are scattered among the dust of the earth and then there are others which bear fruit, to very varying degrees.' Then he adds: 'Don't ask me the reason for this diversity. It is difficult to say. Many elements are at play in determining the result: the quality of the seed and the land, exposure to sun and water. Such comparisons apart, things complicate the outcome in real life. It involves the freedom of each person and his or her willingness to welcome a word which comes from the silence of the mystery. The Father in heaven doesn't force anyone's hand. He has given freedom and responsibility to everyone. He respects both to the very limits of love.'

The disciples were left feeling uneasy. They were looking for a list of accountability, with the goodwill given to the one who would have been willing to change something if he had found it in his means to do so. And Jesus plunges them into a new and disconcerting experience where the accounts never balance and the ways of thinking are so very different from those with which we seek to face our everyday problems.

Jesus strikes the iron until it is hot. He has finally found the right occasion to share with his disciples some of the things closest to his heart.

'You want to know how one foresees the results of working to spread the Gospel. You are right: every worker has the right to an exact pay packet.

But the rules which apply in this instance are very different from the normal ones.

Let's return to the story that I have told you. It helps to speak in concrete terms about things that would otherwise be very difficult to communicate.

You know very well what happens to the grain of wheat when it is sown. It disappears among the clods of earth. Then, with the first watering, it rots and dies. The grain of wheat must die beneath the ground in order to become an ear of corn. If one digs to find it, it is very hard work to discover it. It is no longer as it was before. The farmer is happy. He knows that death is the sure beginning of life.

You see how the perspectives differ. One could say: everything is finished because it is dead. And instead one must rejoice in saying: it is dead therefore it will live. It is flowering into a rich and abundant ear of corn.

This is the peculiar logic of the kingdom of God.

Whoever proclaims it looks for the results. He is right. But the question is this: what results? If you are looking for accolades and if you worry about making converts, you are like the grain of wheat that does not accept that it must die. It will remain but a single grain, and you can bid farewell to any bread for the hungry.'

Jesus' words meet with a long silence. This way of seeing things really disturbs them. The question remains: 'So, how did it go?' The replies are different from those first given. They are a little ashamed. But Jesus smiles. He loves his disciples; he considers them his closest friends, those to whom he will entrust his lifelong mission.

'I'll tell you something else', Jesus insists. 'Think of yeast. Whoever makes bread mixes it in carefully with the flour. The yeast disappears into the flour. It is so hidden that it is no longer visible. And yet, working in secret, it ferments everything. In the morning the dough has risen, ready to become bread.

The word that you preach is like yeast. It seems lost, useless, unproductive. Then the miracle of the bread takes place and the tables of the poor are filled with joy.'

The example of the yeast consoles them. 'Jesus, thank you. We prefer the story of the yeast to that of the seed. Death makes us afraid: it is better to think of the bread that flourishes by a mysterious force which has been buried within the flour. You have chosen us as yeast for the hunger of the world. You change our concerns: help us to become a true handful of yeast.'

Some days later, they return to the question. He has really struck home and made an impression on them. One of them says: 'Now I understand what Jesus was wanting to get across when he told us, in no uncertain terms: after you have done all that you must do, have the courage to recognise that you are only servants.' 'It really is true', says another. 'It wasn't going well for me. To make oneself be the servant... I would have looked away. It really is true. We are servants of the Word. The Father causes life to come forth from our words. We must proclaim it with courage, strength and effectiveness, and aim to be like yeast: to disappear so as to work the better.' All of a sudden Jesus reappears: 'Find the courage to call things by their name: to die in order to give life. Never forget it: in order to give life to all it is necessary to be like the grain of wheat which dies.'

DO NOT BE AFRAID

It had been an afternoon to remember, one of those that leaves a mark.

Jesus had spoken to a massive crowd. They filled every corner of the field, along the gentle slope towards the lake. Those who had succeeded in taking the front rows had found great delight in the discourse given by Jesus. 'We have a Father who loves us. He takes care of us, without demanding anything in return. He counts the hairs on our head and each day he feeds the birds of air.' The others, seated further away, had had to content themselves with a few words, carried by the evening breeze, and with the applause of those who were more fortunate.

The apostles were among the more fortunate ones: seated at Jesus' feet, not missing anything that was said.

But that evening the gathering had ended in the most

unthinkable way. Before saying farewell, Jesus had offered bread and cooked fish. He hadn't minded the expense. Everyone ate their fill. Someone had even managed to make provision for the return. Few knew from whence that gift of God came. Once again the apostles were among the fortunate ones, witnesses to the incredible: five or six loaves, offered by a brave and perceptive boy had fed ten thousand people.

After the final greeting, a few words by way of comment and a long farewell, Jesus had arranged to meet his apostles on the other shore of the lake. 'Aren't you coming?', they had asked him. 'How are you going to join us? We're taking the boat. What about you?' Jesus had been ready with his reply, so evasive that it invited them not to persist: 'Don't worry. I will see to it. I need a little silence and peace. You go. I am staying to pray for a couple of hours and then I'll join you.'

'Be quick'. And they left.

All of a sudden a very strong wind begins to blow. The waves billow. The Sea of Galilee is shaken by one of those freak storms that put fear into even the most experienced fishermen.

The disciples were people of the lake, used to every type of storm. But this is terrifying. The boat is unmanageable, tossed about by the wind and the heavy sea. They do not succeed in turning back and the other shore is too far to reach in this sort of sea.

Someone remarks: 'What a pity, the evening had seemed so calm. It had begun so well. A success. They applauded Jesus as never before. But the final event, paying attention to the hunger of those present and the offer of something to relieve it, that was amazing! It was a great success! And now... What is happening? At least if Jesus was here he would have the right words to comfort us.' They console themselves by thinking of him: 'Perhaps he would even be able to calm the wind and quell the seas.' Peter, the fisherman who was used to treating the sea like a work –

mate and companion, trembles with fear just like the others. He cries out with every breath in his body: 'Jesus, where are you?'

Suddenly, the shadows of the night allow them to catch a glimpse of a distant figure. It moves. It walks on the surface of the water, riding the stormy waves. It draws near to the boat.

'A ghost: someone who drowned on a night like this who is coming to welcome us so that he takes us with him into the kingdom of the dead.' 'Jesus, where are you? Help us, Jesus, save us!'

The shadowy figure is now very near the boat. The last cry died in the throat.

A very gentle voice pierces the sound of the thunder and the waves: 'It is I, do not be afraid. I have come to you. I cannot leave my disciples in danger.'

They do not believe it. There is only a short distance between Jesus and the boat, in the powerful tossing of the waves; the voice is unmistakable. They do not believe it: a dream, the final mirage before shipwreck.

Even Peter finds it hard to recognise Jesus. 'It cannot be him. We left him on the shore without any boat.' It seems like him. It is his voice. But it isn't him.

'If it is really you, call me by my name and I will swim over to you.' 'Peter, jump in and come to me.' Peter does not think twice. He dives in. He is turned over by the waves. He doesn't succeed in keeping afloat, he who had even dared to take to the boats in bad weather. 'Jesus, I am drowning, save me.' 'Peter, have courage, give me your hand. That's it, trust me. Think how many times I gave you good reason to trust me. Why are you still afraid?'

Jesus' hand raises Peter from the waves of the sea. They are aboard the boat: Jesus and Peter together. The disciples look around. They have no more doubts: it really is him. Now they are sure of it.

The wind suddenly drops. Within a few moments the sea is calm. The boat, steered by a mysterious presence, reaches land on the opposite shore of the lake. They have arrived.

Truly an afternoon and a night to remember.

The days go by quickly under the pressing turn of events. The story of the ghost and the boat tossed about by the stormy sea is soon forgotten. They have agreed not to talk about it any more. 'It is better to forget the bad experience. Never mind the fear: the stormy sea frightens everyone. Even if we joked about it the first time we told the story. To have taken Jesus for a ghost – we who had spent many months cheek by jowl with him – this is the limit. Let's forget about it and woe betide anyone who mentions it.'

Then the sad days came. They arrested Jesus. They tried, condemned and killed him. His enemies triumphed. The disciples ran away. Fear returns: a terrible experience which cancels out all the happy memories at a stroke. The stormy sea and the ghost walking calmly across the waves. Now everything has truly ended in the worst possible way. 'Jesus, where are you?' The poor disciples no longer have even the strength to shout this out.

That evening, gathered in a room shut off from the outside, they thought once more about the boat tossed by the wind: 'Jesus would like it here.' Sadly, he is no more. They had overcome and destroyed him. They too were finished: their dreams had been buried in the tomb with their master.

But it is not finished. Jesus returns victorious. This time he does not calm the raging sea. He encourages the disciples with the power of his Spirit and sends them to the four corners of the earth. At last they have changed: transformed within. The encounter with the Risen One has worked the miracle. They have no more fear.

They are rushing to speak to Jesus with a zeal that they would never have dreamed of having. They speak loudly and make brave gestures. The records of the first Christian community report a few fragments of the discourse. The words with which Peter defends the healing of the lame man at the Beautiful Gate of the temple: 'Do you want to know why this lame man now walks firm and upright? Be it known to all of you and the whole people of Israel: in the name of Jesus Christ the Nazarene, whom you crucified and whom God raised from the dead, by him this man stands in front of you well and saved. This Jesus is the stone which, rejected by you builders, has become the cornerstone. There is salvation in no one else: in fact, there is no other name under heaven given to men by which we can be saved' (Acts 4:9-12).

Every so often they return to the bad experience of the lake and the ghost. 'It was a moment of weakness. We cannot be ashamed of it. On the contrary, it must be remembered: even in this way we can think of Jesus' presence in our life.' They all agree: it is one of those special moments to tell whoever will believe in Jesus through their preaching. They think: who knows how many other people will be tempted not to acknowledge Jesus in life's difficult moments? And they conclude: 'If we ourselves have come through this sad episode, we who really couldn't be mistaken after all the proof that Jesus gave us, then our story can serve to comfort and sustain. Let it be told.'

Paul had experienced it at first hand. He gives us a very beautiful comment about it: 'So as to keep me from being too elated by the wealth of revelations, I have been given a thorn in the flesh, a messenger of Satan charged with harassing me, to prevent me from being too elated. Because of this I besought the Lord three times, that it should leave me. And he said to me: my grace is enough for you; in fact, my power is shown to the full in weakness. I will all the more willingly boast of my weaknesses, that the power of Christ may rest upon me. For the sake of Christ, therefore, I am happy with weaknesses, insults, hardships, persecutions and calamities: when I am weak, it is then that I am strong.' (2 Cor 12:7-10).

IF YOUR HEART IS TROUBLED

'I am afraid that tonight I will be alone, surrounded only by my enemies.'

It is sad to remain alone, abandoned by everyone. And it is all the more disconcerting to discover that the traitors are nestling among one's friends.

'Tonight you will desert me. I will be betrayed by one of you.' Jesus' words, painful and compassionate, fall upon the disciples who have gathered to eat the festive meal. They are speechless, disturbed and sad. Is it possible? To betray Jesus? To abandon him after all he has been for each of them. 'Why should we do that?' they ask one another. 'Out of fear' Jesus adds. His enemies were ready. They had decided everything. They have had enough. They will come armed to the teeth, their minds made up: now or never.

'You will give me up to them. Indeed, one of you will even take their side, for fear of meeting the same end as me.'

Peter has had enough. He bursts out, as sure of himself as ever. 'Jesus, not this. I will not betray you, never. Rest assured: even if everyone were to forsake you, not I. I cannot do it. You are everything to me. I have left everything to be with you! Would you that at the most critical moment I should change my mind?'

'Peter... we too... all of us. Never, no never... Jesus, stay calm... we will stay with you even if it costs us our lives.' This is what they all say, to a man.

Jesus is silent. The discussion changes. They return to their feasting. A few hours go by and Jesus' fears are realised. He is alone in the garden. He prays to his Father, exhausted by the menace that weighs upon him. He prays and sweats blood. The others, his disciples, even the most faithful, sleep peacefully, weakened by fatigue and emotion.

Then, all of a sudden, the soldiers arrive. Jesus is arrested and brought before the tribunal.

The disciples run away. The weak resistance is controlled by Jesus himself, ready to forgive even at the last moment.

Peter wanders around Jerusalem by night, desperate. Then he reaches the courtyard of the tribunal. Up above, amidst unseemly shouting, Jesus is being tried. Down below, around the fire, Peter is waiting. He wants to know how things will end, but he has no intention of letting himself be recognised. He doesn't want to risk it. He has already begun to draw aside, he who a few hours before had declared himself ready for everything for the sake of his master.

A woman comes up. She doesn't have any pretensions. She knows that she counts for little among this circle of men who are warming themselves by the fire and discussing the day's events. The poor thing, she is only a maidservant. She must be careful: not to say too much of what she has heard, otherwise they can make her lose her job.

First of all she listens. Then she asks them a question. Perhaps it is only out of curiosity or trying to be noticed. It is certainly not an accusation. For goodness sake... she could not really allow herself to do that.

'Listen, Peter, that Jesus whom they are condemning, do you know him? You have associated with him, haven't you? What is he like?' Peter is scared out of his wits: 'I have never seen him: whatever makes you think that? What kind of question are you asking me? Please, are we being serious?'

The woman is not convinced. She stops and listens. Peter has started speaking like a river in full flood. He wants to show that he doesn't really have anything to do with Jesus.

The woman insists: 'It is hard to imagine that you don't know him. You speak like him. You have the same tone of voice. I bet that you come from the same place. Is it possible that you don't know him?'

This time Peter has had enough. His throat is tightened with fear. 'That's enough', he shouts, 'leave off. You are talking nonsense. I have never set eyes on that man Jesus.'

Peter's outburst proves counterproductive. Some others seem to confirm the woman's claim. Peter swears an oath and lies: 'I do not know who Jesus is. I have never seen him. They should condemn him if he deserves it. They should let him go if he has done nothing serious. I don't know. It doesn't matter to me. And leave it there, once and for all. You are annoying me.'

He gets up to go. He wants to show that he is right. They have offended him and he goes off.

He had only gone a few steps and he finds himself surrounded by deathly despair.

'I have betrayed him. I have betrayed Jesus. I have betrayed him because I am a coward. It didn't cost me anything and I betrayed him. And now what will I do? Where can I run? I have betrayed my Lord. I myself have condemned him to death.'

He stops. Someone is coming down the steps. It is Jesus, surrounded by soldiers and bound like a criminal. He has been condemned twice: by the perverse judgement and by his friend's betrayal.

Peter looks at Jesus. The final look and then he does not stay until the death of this desperate man.

Jesus looks at Peter. A look of kindness: a deeply welcoming embrace. He had never experienced it like tonight. Jesus put his arms around his neck... he, Peter, who betrayed him out of fear.

Their glances met very quickly. There was not even time for a word. He didn't even manage to call out 'Jesus'. The soldiers led him away, pushing and pulling him.

Peter stays there for the time being. Jesus' look speaks volumes.

He hears the distant echo of a very beautiful story which Jesus had told some months before. He hadn't understood it very well then. It seemed strange to him, too submissive. Now he discovered everything anew: it is his story.

'A man had two sons. The youngest said to his father: Father, give me the part of the inheritance which belongs to

147

me. And the father divides the property between them. After a few days the youngest son gathers his belongings, and he left for a far-off land. There he squandered his wealth by living a dissolute life. When everything had been spent, a great famine came upon that land and he began to find himself in need. Then he came to his senses and said: How many servants there are in my father's house who have plenty of bread, and here am I dying of hunger. I will get up and go back to my father and I will say to him: Father, I have sinned against heaven and against you; I am not worthy to be called your son. Treat me like one of your house-boys. He left and set off towards his father's house. While he was still a long way off, his father saw him and moved with compassion he ran to meet him. He threw his arms around his neck and kissed him. The son said to him: Father, I have sinned against heaven and against you; I am no longer worthy to be called your son. But the father said to his servants: Make haste, bring the finest clothes and put them on him, put a ring on his finger and shoes on his feet. Bring a fatted calf, kill it, and let's eat and make merry, because this son of mine was dead and has come back to life, he was lost and has been found. And they began to feast' (Lk 15:11-32).

The story has transformed him. The smile returns to his face. He is no longer afraid. Jesus' embrace has destroyed his sin. He has gone back to what he was like before, with an experience which has changed him inside and through which he has been touched by God's welcoming love.

One day he had asked Jesus: 'You say to forgive. And I agree. But you have not said how many times it is necessary to forgive. How many times?' Jesus does not suggest any numbers. He says to Peter: 'Do what I urge you to do: be generous. You never can tell.' Peter was testing to the limit the greatest generosity that seemed possible. 'Jesus, seven times, is that enough?' He was expecting Jesus to rebuke him: 'That's too much. Hold on, Peter, sin cannot be dealt with rashly.'

Jesus scolds him for the opposite reason: 'Too little.

One always forgives. Everything can be forgiven, without any limit of time and number. It is enough to trust God's love and entrust oneself to him, like a baby in its mother's arms.' 'Remember', Jesus insists, 'even if a mother could forget her child, God never forgets us.'

Even in that situation, Peter remained doubtful. And what if Jesus had been exaggerating a little? Now everything is revealed. His betrayal... more than seven times. It alone is equal to all the sins of the world.

Jesus, with one glance, envelops him in his welcoming love. With a countenance by now transformed by blows and spittle, he says: 'Peter, have courage, let's have a feast. I had lost you and now you are mine, forever.'

Peter runs out of the tribunal courtyard. He looks for his friends. He gathers them together. In one breath he tells them his about his betrayal. He is happy. He is not out of his mind. He has been touched by Jesus' forgiving hand, he who would have deserved the most severe punishment.

Someone advised him to remain silent. 'Peter, do not say anything. You cut a very bad figure. Let's forget all about it: let's pretend nothing has happened. We assure you that we too will keep quiet. The Church would get off to a very bad start. Excuse us for saying, but you know that Jesus entrusted you with a very great responsibility: you have a dignity to be respected.'

Peter is of the opposite mind. He does not manage to keep silent. He tells everyone: 'I betrayed the master in the worst possible way. And he threw his arms around me. I am the young man who ran away from home, whom the father envelops in his welcoming embrace. We must tell everyone. I have felt the warmth of the most beautiful news in my life.'

He did so much and spoke so much that, on the contrary, they had to record the event in the Gospel texts. It was too important to forget about. The most beautiful comment was reserved, much later, to John, in the Letter written to the Christian community very many years after the death of

Jesus: 'Even if our hearts condemn us, God is greater than our hearts' (1 Jn 3:20).

A SCHOOL OF PRAYER

They had placed so much hope in it. They had accepted Jesus' invitation with enthusiasm. They had left everything to follow him, captivated by his personality and convinced of his aims.

But now everything appeared to have come to an end, and in the worst possible way.

Jesus' enemies had arrested him. They had subjected him to a trial which was all a sham. They had condemned him like a criminal, he who had only done good to all those he had met. Then, after having tortured him, they had killed him. And so everything had come to an end. Jesus had promised to overcome even death. He had done so for others. But for himself nothing of the kind. Jesus had been obliterated from the sight and hearts of his friends. His enemies had triumphed. Everything must go back to how it had been before.

Never mind: it had been a lovely dream, over too soon and in the most tragic way.

Now there was really nothing more to do. It was necessary to return home, with the sadness of nostalgia and a little shame. It was necessary to take up one's work tools, so readily abandoned a few months before.

To go back to how things were before: as if nothing had happened, overcoming even the mocking smile of those who were once friends, who had not understood the strange wish to follow that man from Nazareth who had been making a lot of enemies with his ideas.

Many disciples had already taken the road home. Now it affected them as well. Fair enough, they decided to return to Emmaus, to their own homes, as if nothing had happened. They were walking along, exchanging a few sad words. They had no others: the last ones had left them choked – the sad farewell to their friends who were staying behind in Jerusalem.

All of a sudden, a wayfarer came up, appearing as if from nowhere. Like them he had come from the direction of Jerusalem. But they hadn't noticed him before.

'Good day.' 'Greetings.' 'Where are you going?' 'We have come from Jerusalem and we are going home to Emmaus. It's not far now, thank goodness.'

The pilgrim asks: 'May I join you? I am going there as well. It's a long road and, in these times, a little dangerous too. May we go along together?'

'Good grief, what sad faces you have! I hadn't noticed it before. You seem to me as if you have just come from a funeral. Am I mistaken?'

The reply was immediate. The words flowed like a flood of tears. 'We really have come from a funeral. It's the talk of Jerusalem. How come you don't know about it? They killed Jesus of Nazareth. He was our friend and master. We were with him, we shared his zeal for the liberation of Israel and his hope in the future of God. They put him to death, nailed to the cross, after a trial that seemed set to condemn him on purpose.'

There was a pause to take a breath and to recall the last rays of that hope which had enflamed their hearts.

'He had done nothing but good: he healed the sick, treated the poor well, had a good word even for sinners. He even raised the dead. You have surely heard about Lazarus, the one from Bethany. Jesus brought him back to life three days after he died. Alas, he spoke too freely about God and the law. He loved the poor people too much.

'They killed him. Who? Surely you know! The Romans, but with the complicity of our priests and doctors of the law.'

'Before he died, he promised that he too would return to

life, like his friend Lazarus. But by now three days have gone by and nothing has happened.'

The second disciple added: 'Nothing indeed: that is not true! You know, there were also some women in our circle. They stayed with us to serve Jesus. A pair of them say they have seen Jesus risen from the dead. No one believes them. They are fanatics. If they imagined it, you accept out of sorrow and love.'

'His closest friends, Peter and the others, have seen nothing.'

'It's all over. We too are going home.'

'Keep calm. Don't jump to conclusions', replies their strange travelling companion. 'You are interpreting events incorrectly. You stop at what you have seen with your eyes. I am sorry for you: you are a little blind. You do not know how to interpret events from within.'

'Help us then, if you can.' 'With pleasure. Listen.'

Step by step they draw closer to their homes. Step by step their travelling companion helps them to reinterpret events in terms of the mystery they contain within. He cites passages from the Scriptures. He recalls old and new prophecies. He brings distant memories into the present.

Not even when they were with Jesus had they experienced anything like this. Then they were all geared towards the future. They had almost forgotten the past. The present and its plans were too important to think about the past.

Now, however, they go towards the past from the present. They understand it anew, immersing it into the mystery of God. The marvellous deeds done by God for his people become a new way of interpreting the present. Even darkness, uncertainty and sadness change in style. They are penetrated with the light of something never before discovered.

They look each other in the eye. 'It is strange, but they did not kill our hope. They had exhausted it. They had tried to extinguish it and we had fallen into the trap. Were it not for our present experience it was becoming desperate. We were returning home because we were without a future. Instead, there is hope. Jesus was right when he spoke about the grain of wheat that must die in order to become an ear of corn.'

'They killed him but they have not triumphed. God overcomes death. It was all part of God's mysterious plan.' The words of the psalms fall from their lips spontaneously. They have a new flavour. They had never been aware of them before.

'And if we were to return to Jerusalem?' 'Tomorrow. It is late now. We cannot make the journey at night. It is too dangerous. Tomorrow.'

By now they had reached the outskirts of Emmaus. They arrived at their destination: tomorrow morning, at first light, they go back to Jerusalem.

Their travelling companion made as to bid them farewell in order to continue on his way. 'Are you going on? At this hour?' They insist: 'Stop here with us. We'll have no problem finding a place for you in our house. Go on, stay.'

They had resigned themselves to going back to their former lives. They had rowed the oars of their boat, disheartened and frustrated. But the experience of Jesus had left a mark on them. They had truly taken in the need to show hospitality. Their words were not simply dictated by circumstances. They came from the heart. 'Stay with us. You are our guest.'

The mysterious traveller stays. There was some resistance, perhaps to know how genuine was the invitation. Then he stops and accepts the gesture of hospitality.

They sit down at table.

At a particular point their eyes are opened.

Jesus had been walking with them. He had prayed with them along the road, helping them to interpret events from the mystery they bore within. He had helped them to pray in contemplation.

Now that prayer breaks out into celebration. Jesus takes the bread and the cup of wine. He blesses and distributes it.

There is a cry: 'It is him, the crucified and risen one. How is it possible that we were not aware of it before? We were well and truly blind, with sorrow and resignation.'

He is no longer there. He is gone in the silence from which he came.

The few hours spent with him have left their mark. He has led them by hand through an intense experience of prayer, which has changed them profoundly.

Their faint-heartedness is overpowered by the return of hope and zeal. Prayer and celebration open them to life. Now it is not too late to go back to Jerusalem. There are no longer any dangers on the journey by night. They set off with haste: they are going to tell the others about this experience.

They return to Jerusalem, to proclaim to everyone: Jesus is risen, his great adventure for the life and hope of everyone continues. On the contrary: it is beginning again.

BIBLICAL TEXTS

The stories told in this book are all inspired by a biblical text. When the reference is given, the expressions are derived from the letter of the text. As a rule, I have preferred not to give the direct quotation, to avoid all incorrect usage of Scripture. Instead I invite the reader to make personal contact with the biblical text, to challenge my interpretation and, above all, to meditate upon the Word of the Lord. To make this a little easier, I give the main references which have inspired me in telling the stories which follow.

A school of prayer
Luke 24:13-35

A significant experience
Luke 9:23-36

Can we write new 'Letters to Philemon'?
Philemon

Do not be afraid
Mark 6:45-52

Education in the law
John 8:1-11

Enough of materialism
Matthew 19:16-29; 20:20-28

Faithful to the cause
Mark 3:31-35; John 19:26-27

How did it go?
Mark 4:1-20

If your heart is troubled
Luke 15:11-32; 22:54-62

In favour of life – but how?
Luke 20:9-19; John 6:1-14

In the service of life
Luke 9:49-50

Looking to the future
Matthew 25:1-13

Peter, the man who was lame and the message of Jesus
Acts 3:1-9;4:1-11

Planning the way ahead
Luke 9:37-43

Read within
Matthew 11:2-6

Real problems
Mark 5:21-43; Luke 21:1-4

Self-giving love
Luke 10:25-37

Signs of faith
John 20:24-29

Thank you, Nicodemus
John 3:1-21

The Council of Jerusalem
Acts 15:1-21

The joy of following Jesus
Matthew 10:5-15; Luke 9:57-62; Luke 5:27-32

Wanting to separate good from evil
Matthew 13:24-30

Ways of seeing things
2 Samuel 12:1-14

Who is the human person?
Luke 18:9-14

Who is the strongest?
Matthew 18:1-5; John 18:19-24

Whose side are you on, God?
Luke 13;10-17

Wishing to see Jesus
Luke 19:1-10